UNDERSTANDING LEADERSHIP

▶▶▶▶▶▶▶▶▶▶▶▶▶▶▶▶▶▶▶▶▶▶▶

*Fresh Perspectives on the
Essentials of New
Testament Leadership*

Tom Marshall

Emerald
Books

P.O. Box 635
Lynnwood, Washington 98046

Published by Emerald Books
P.O. Box 635
Lynnwood, Washington 98046
USA

Published in agreement with:
Sovereign World Ltd.
P.O. Box17
Chichester PO20 6YB
England

ISBN 0-92754-551-9

Typeset by CRB Typesetting Services, Ely, Cambs,
England
Printed in the USA

Contents

Foreword		3
Introduction.	What is Leadership?	5
Chapter 1.	Foresight, the Leader's Lead	9
Chapter 2.	Goals – The Leader's Aim	20
Chapter 3.	The Question of Timing	30
Chapter 4.	Imparting the Vision	35
Chapter 5.	Danger – Power at Work	42
Chapter 6.	The Redemption of Power	55
Chapter 7.	The Redemption of Leadership	66
Chapter 8.	How to Become a Servant Leader	74
Chapter 9.	The Status Syndrome	82
Chapter 10.	Coping With Criticism	91
Chapter 11.	Authority – The Leader's Mantle	100
Chapter 12.	Biblical Stress Management	114
Chapter 13.	Relationships – The Leader's Network	130
Chapter 14.	Trust, the Cost of Commitment	145
Chapter 15.	Who Cares? Love and Leadership	160
Chapter 16.	Made for Honour	170
Chapter 17.	Understanding Understanding	179
Chapter 18.	Meet the Corporation	192
Chapter 19.	The City Revisited	203
Chapter 20.	When Leaders Fail	212

Foreword

It was early one morning when I received the call at my Surrey home from Tom Marshall. The line was so clear due to our modern technology I had imagined he was somewhere up the road in London. In reality he was in New Zealand. 'Would you write a foreword for my book, *Understanding Leadership*?'

I hesitated not a second. Superlatives were in abundance. Tom Marshall has to my mind been one of New Zealand's best kept secrets.

His teaching ability, the easy readability and access to his perspectives along with his quite refreshing non-religious style, are all quite unique. His writings have fed, educated and challenged my thinking for years. My several tours of New Zealand have allowed me to gain first-hand testimonies of those who both feel and know the same as I do about Tom Marshall.

As for this book, the blue pencil will have to deal with the clutch of superlatives that are likely to surface from my pen. Sufficient to say that I shall be taking it upon myself to ensure that all leaders in our Pioneer network of churches in the UK each receive a copy. I want them not only to read it but prayerfully discuss and respond to its illuminating nature, practical application and rich breadth, consistently hinting that the writer has a long and deep experience of his subject.

The price of the publication is worth it just for the chapter entitled 'The Status Syndrome'. Or you may find that the chapter on 'Coping with Criticism' or 'Biblical Stress Management' or the quite brilliant 'When Leaders Fail' make the book so valuable for leaders and aspiring leaders. God himself is going to speak through these pages from different chapters. He has his eye on leaders and intends to help them.

Within the Body of Christ God has given us thinkers, writers, speakers, singers and doers. Those who think biblically and creatively are not always so good at oration or indeed knowing what to do about what they think! Likewise the doers of our age don't always think things through despite their obvious 'doing' skills and expertise. But be encouraged. Moses heard from God but Aaron preached his sermons! This is body ministry! Leaders need one another.

Life begins with us being totally dependent on others. We grow up and of necessity go through a phase of independence. This is the time when we discover who we are, what we can do and (if are wise) what our limitations are. But interdependence is a higher value than either dependence or independence.

The chapters in this book put relationships at the heart of everything. Relationship with God. Relationship with one another. It nurtures and fosters interpendence whilst maintaining identity and integrity. This will create a high trust climate.

In my own autobiography *An Intelligent Fire* I stated 'I'm a generalist but I am what I am today because I have surrounded myself with specialists'. Tom Marshall specialises in the uncanny knack of going to the root of leadership problems and then lovingly but scripturally applying sensible Godly remedies.

The publication will make for a healthy body of believers fed and taught by a healthy body of leaders. That is why I want every leader and aspiring leader to read this book.

Gerald Coates
Leader Pioneer Team
Esher, Surrey

Introduction

What is Leadership?

A couple of years ago when passing through Los Angeles I picked a newspaper off the airport bookstand. In it was a report of a conference of trustees and managers from more than 1,000 of America's most elite institutions, the group of large philanthropic foundations whose purpose is to give away money. The theme of their three day conference was 'Exploring the many dimensions of leadership'.

The conclusions the conference came to were startling. There was, they agreed, nothing less than a crisis of leadership in American society; the nation was being guided, not by leaders but by managers and its condition could be described as being over-managed and under-led! 'What is more,' said the newspaper report, 'This prophesying came, not from wild eyed Jeremiahs, but from serious and successful Americans including the owner of a metropolitan newspaper, an eminent scholar and one of the directors of the world's largest corporation.'

The findings of this conference have been chosen as a point of departure for this study, for two good reasons. One is that they point to a current modern malaise, the serious shortage of good leaders in most of the institutions of our society, including the Christian church. The other is that they suggest one of the reasons for that lack, the presence of considerable confusion and uncertainty, both as to what is meant by this business of leadership, and how you actually go about doing it. Thus the two questions we will hope to address, are the ones that should be in the forefront of every seeker after understanding and knowledge about anything

1. What does it actually mean?
2. How do you do it?

Leadership and management

Most books and seminars on leadership assume that the essence of the subject is already well known and the basis of it generally agreed upon by the readers or seminar participants. Thus they tend to deal largely with the refinements of the craft, or the ways of improving leadership performance by the use of organisation theory and management technology. It is no wonder then if leaders get the message that to lead effectively you must be a good administrator and learn to use the manager's techniques, or that managers using the tools they are familiar with, think that in so doing they are leading.

It is true, of course, that you can have a leader who is also a good manager, or a manager who is a leader, but the two functions are quite different and must not be confused. Management is essentially the stewardship of resources and its concern is with making the organisation work effectively and efficiently. To do this it involves itself with logistics, information, people and systems; it builds teams, controls budgets, measures performance, monitors progress, and initiates corrective action where needed. These operating functions are vital to the success of the venture but they have nothing essentially to do with leadership. You can use every one of them and yet not be leading at all, you are merely reacting to situations as they arise. Conversely you may lead effectively and yet not be involved in any of these operational or managerial activities. Leadership in other words is not management and it is not administration.

Leadership and ministry

Another mistake, and the one most often made in the Christian church, is to equate leadership with ministry. The leader,

6

whether minister, pastor or elder, is therefore expected to be the best preacher, the best bible teacher, the best counsellor, the best prophet and the best organiser in the church. Very often the minister places the same expectations on himself, because that is how he has been trained to think. As a consequence he feels threatened if gifts arise in the congregation that appear to threaten his supremacy in any area of ministry, particularly the one he favours most. Gifted people in the church are thus either ignored or shut out of opportunities to exercise their gifts until they become frustrated and discontented. Sometimes the more independent ones eventually go off and start out on their own, when they are then accused of being rebellious or divisive.

If, as a church leader, I find among my flock, someone who is a better preacher or a better bible teacher than I am, I should welcome the gift. If someone arises who is a better counsellor or a better evangelist or a better organiser than I am, I should heartily rejoice in their capacities and give them scope to grow and flourish. None of the ministry gifts has anything essentially to do with my leadership role or need affect my leadership function in any way. The best and most effective leaders understand this clearly. For example, Count Zinzendorf was the leader of the 18th Century Moravian community in Herrenhut, but the most popular preacher, we read, was an old man who worked as a potter. When the potter was preaching bigger crowds flocked to hear him than to hear Zinzendorf, but there is no record of the Count being envious of the potter's reputation or feeling threatened thereby.

The heart of leadership

What then is the essence or the essential heart of this thing we call leadership? In other words, what are the features that distinguish leaders from other people in the organisation, and the leadership role from other roles or functions? Are there common factors that apply generally to all expressions of leadership?

7

Unless we get this fundamental understanding right we may be building a lot of leadership training and skills on faulty foundations, cluttering up leaders with methods and procedures that have little or nothing to do with their function, or trying to superimpose leadership models on people who are not leaders and will never be leaders.

In the section that follows we will go immediately to the heart of the matter and identify the capacities and characteristics that are critical to the whole leadership function regardless of the organisation and regardless of the level within the organisation structure.

Chapter 1

Foresight, the Leader's Lead

Goals – heading towards the future

The first essential characteristic of leaders is that they are going somewhere, in other words they are aiming at goals or objectives that lie in the future. Their interest therefore is in what is to come rather than in what is past, in the possibilities and opportunities that lie on the time horizon rather than the things that have already been accomplished. Leaders, in other words, are always on the way, they are heading towards objectives, aiming at targets and reaching out for things that are ahead of them.

Thus John writes about the good shepherd,

> *'He calls his own sheep by name and leads them out. When he has brought out all his own, he goes on ahead of them, and his sheep follow him because they know his voice.'* John 10:4 NIV

The shepherd is 'leading' because he is out in front. He is going somewhere, therefore he has gone ahead to show the way. The sheep are simply following the 'lead' of the shepherd.

The first question therefore to be asked of all leaders is 'What are your goals?' If leaders are not aiming at something but are merely responding or reacting to situations as they arise, they have already virtually surrendered leadership. Circumstances or situations are leading the way and effectively determining what is going to be done. The role of the leaders has become a maintenance or an operational one, because their attention is focused on the present and the past, rather than on the future.

I would go a step further, I would want to know whether the leaders had goals for their private and personal life as well as for their public and institutional life. The private area was the one the early church always looked at when assessing whether a man had the qualities of leadership. If he could not lead and take care of his own family, they reasoned, how could he be trusted to lead and take care of God's church (1 Timothy 3:5)?

Foresight – Dealing with the Future

Being future oriented is a necessary requirement for leadership, but it is not a sufficient requirement. In other words, although leaders need to have goals, they need to be much more than merely goal-directed. People who are not leaders also need goals, they also need to be going somewhere.

What distinguishes leaders from others is that they not only have an interest in the future they also have the capacity to deal with the future. This capacity is sometimes called 'foresight'. As Robert K. Greenleaf puts it,

> 'A mark of leaders, an attribute that puts them in a position to show the way for others, is that they are better than most at pointing the direction to go. Foresight is the "lead" that the leader has. Once leaders lose this lead and events start to force their hand, they are leaders in name only.'

We need to examine this concept of foresight in more detail because of its unique importance to the whole business of leadership. There are other leadership qualities that are also necessary or desirable, but none is as vital to the leadership function, particularly at the higher levels, as foresight. Its absence will sooner or later derail an otherwise well qualified and well equipped encumbent of a leadership position.

What then is involved in this ability or capacity to deal effectively with the future that we call foresight?

Firstly, foresight requires vision, in the sense of imaginative insight or 'seeing' with the inner eye. It may be, but is not necessarily, visualisation, that is, actually seeing pictures in the mind's eye. It is more commonly experienced in the form of ideas or concepts or thoughts but it is still vision. Vision is what enables leaders to 'see' the possible future further and more clearly than others, to be better than others at identifying opportunities and possibilities, and knowing how to respond to forthcoming events or likely situations. Vision is an essential hallmark of all the great leaders, it marks out a Moses or a Joshua, a Samuel or a David or a Nehemiah.

Secondly, foresight consists of a sense for the unknown, an instinctive 'feel' or anticipatory prescience for what is not here yet, an intuitive kind of knowledge or awareness of things prior to their existence or occurrence. It is therefore largely a spiritual capacity and one that, from a Christian perspective, carries with it the potential for, or the openness to inspiration or revelation. (1 Corinthians 2:9–13)

If leadership requires an orientation towards the future, a capacity for vision and an openness to inspiration, then clearly the Christian community should be able to produce more and better leaders than any other section of human society. To begin with, we are future oriented, we are the people who belong to the future and to whom the future belongs because we belong to the Lord who holds the future. It is the gods of this age who are on their way out. (1 Corinthians 2:6) Furthermore, we are the people upon whom the Holy Spirit has been poured out, with the specific promise that our young men would see visions and our old men would dream dreams.

The Christian church ought therefore to be turning out, in great numbers, men and women who can become leaders in, and give direction to all the major institutions of our societies. The great question today is whether there exists in the Christian church a sufficient reservoir of spiritual strength with the capacity to throw up leaders of the right calibre to meet the challenge of the present leadership vacuum. This is a major question to which we will have to return more than once before we are through with this study.

The Features of Foresight

If foresight is a spiritual capacity, it may be thought to defy rational analysis, but in fact many of its features can be readily described. This is important so that we can recognise how foresight works and can therefore identify its presence either in ourselves or in others.

Spiritual Aspects

From a spiritual perspective, that is at the level of the human spirit, we can isolate the following characteristics:

1. It has certain links and parallels with the prophetic gift, for example, the early Hebrew prophets were called 'seers'. They were, however, not primarily involved with predicting totally unknown future events, they were much more concerned with 'seeing' the future that was latent or potential in the present and its conditions or circumstances.

Thus the prophet comes to a situation in Israel of apparent peace and prosperity, but he perceives or senses the inner departure from God that has taken place in the hearts of the people. Therefore he 'sees' and calls attention to the impending judgment that will certainly come on the land, even though it may be a generation ahead, unless the nation repents now and returns to its covenant commitment with God.

Or the prophet comes to a situation where disillusionment and despair are everywhere, and yet he discerns the almost imperceptible turning of the people's hearts back to God, and the graciousness of God's response. Therefore in the midst of the present blackness he 'sees' the promise of a glorious future restoration in which the nation can already hope and towards which it must even now begin to reorient itself.

2. The exercise of foresight also involves the use of a wider

than usual span of awareness, that is, the person is open to perceptions not only at the factual or sensory levels but also at the level of direct apprehension or intuition. These latter perceptions range across a spectrum from 'hunches' or gut level feelings, to presentiments or shrewd discernments and on to those inputs that are mediated through the gifts of the Holy Spirit such as a word of knowledge or a word of wisdom or that come in the form of dreams or visions.

3. Thirdly, foresight requires the ability to integrate or synthesise these diverse inputs and perceptions so as to come up with a better than average prediction as to what the future may hold and what the appropriate response to it should be. The way in which this integration takes place may be deliberate and studied but it is more often very intuitive and almost instinctive and not really totally understood even by the person doing it. All they can sometimes tell you is that they 'just know' what could happen or where opportunities are going to appear.

This same capacity is possessed by the very small handful of truly outstanding players in any sport, for example the basketball player or football player who has the uncanny knack of always being in the right place at the right time to take the unexpected pass or the unexpected scoring opportunity. They make it all look so very easy but they cannot tell you why they knew to position themselves just at that particular spot at that particular moment or why they could anticipate that play would flow in that direction and not another.

We find another and more complex illustration in the way in which the later prophets in Israel gave advice to the kings on the political situation of the day and its implications for the future of the nation. In developing the insight or foresight on which their prophetic word rested they made use of input and perceptions from at least three distinct sources.

(a) Their own informed and intelligent analysis of the political scene and the state of the empires and alliances of the nations surrounding Israel.

(b) Their knowledge of the character and ways of God, and his way of dealing with Israel as revealed in the prophetic writings.

(c) The immediate oracle or judgment word from God, received as the prophet stood in the council of God and acted as his messenger (Jeremiah 23:22)

This prophetic model is very important because leaders in their leadership role will many times find that they also have to function in the same three simultaneous roles of analyst, historian and prophet.

(a) As analyst they are often required to break the situation or the problem or the organisation down into its component parts so as to understand all the implications or the way the parts relate together to make up the whole.
(b) As historian they have to assess the significance of past precedents and previous experience and the ways in which they affect the understanding of the present circumstances and decisions about the future, and
(c) As prophet their task is to 'see' the future that is latent in the present and to be open to receive creative inspiration as to how best to act.

The Mindset of Foresight

Foresight however also requires certain specific capacities or capabilities at the intellectual or rational level and these need to be consciously applied and developed. We can distinguish the following:

1. Developing a constant and habitual orientation of the mind towards the future. If we are not continually looking for things in the future we will never discover them. To seek and keep on seeking remains the basic condition for finding. (Matthew 7:7)

In any area of vocation or ministry we have to give ourselves to the demands of the particular calling, that is to say, everything must henceforth be seen from the perspective of that calling and be at the service of the calling. For example, part of my role for a good number of years has been as a teacher in the body of Christ, therefore everything that happens to me and everything in which I am involved and everything I see or observe has to be examined and appraised and screened to find out the principles that apply or the lessons that have to be learned. Whatever else they are, all these things are also grist to the mill of my calling as a teacher.

If you are a leader, that is your calling. It demands that you develop a certain mindset. The future, and what may lie in the future, and what you may do in the future is one of the primary perspectives from which you must begin to examine everything that goes on around you.

2. Acquiring the habit of examining everything and assessing everything in terms of potential and possibilities, even if there is never going to be any chance of your making use of it. The questions you should always be asking are:

> 'What could be done with this?
> How could we capitalise on that?
> If I was doing this, how could I do it better than is being done with it at present?
> What unused or unrealised possibilities or opportunities are going begging here?'

Probably only a small percentage of the situations or circumstances you examine will present possibilities and fewer still will be at all feasible. Nevertheless, if you are not always looking for openings, the golden opportunities can slip past unnoticed or will be seen too late to do anything about them.

3. It also involves not only the active gathering of information, data, impressions, opinions, insights and hunches, but with it,

(a) An instinctive sense for what is relevant and what is not,
(b) The ability to see pattern, order and relationships between the facts, and
(c) Often the ability to see singular or unusual connections between seemingly unrelated factors or a higher level of unity or integration amongst dissimilar or disparate data or events.

4. Associated with this is the capacity for creative thinking, that is, the ability to generate possibilities or ideas that make sense of some or all of the information that has been assembled.

Much has been written on ways to tap into the creative levels of the human mind, from brainstorming techniques to lateral thinking, and there are useful pointers to be gleaned from many of the methods suggested, for example:

(a)   The deliberate abandonment of old stereotypes or ways of doing things. The familiar can be a barrier to the new, not because it is wrong but just because it is customary, so we find that God says:

> *'Forget the former things; do not dwell on the past.*
> *See, I am doing a new thing!'*   Isaiah 43:18 NIV

(b)   When the way to the desired goal cannot be found, sometimes it pays to start from the goal and work backwards or from some point in the middle and work both ways. If you can find the way from the middle point to the final goal, all you then have to do is find the way back from the intermediate point to the place you have to start from. You find something of this kind in Exodus chapter 3. God sent Moses to bring the children of Israel out of Egypt to worship God at Sinai, then when they were at Sinai God would lead them to Canaan. Maybe Egypt to Canaan in one leap was more than Moses could conceptualise at that juncture.

(c)   Often new ideas can be generated by cross fertilisation from other unrelated fields or disciplines. The situation can then be examined from an entirely different perspective or seen in a totally different setting. Scripture does this repeatedly, using analogies from athletics, war, anatomy, agriculture and nature to illuminate spiritual truths.

5. Having gathered all the information and data, there is the ability to step back from it within yourself and allow time for

creative inspiration to emerge. That is a discipline of mind and will, brilliantly exemplified by Jesus in John's Gospel. When he was challenged by the carefully set trap of the Pharisees over the woman taken in adultery we read that Jesus stooped and wrote on the ground. What was he doing? He had gathered all the data at his command, the law of Moses, his reputation as a rabbi, his role as the merciful prophet, and he had considered all the implications of all the possible answers he could give. Then he steps back inside himself to receive illumination. Then the creative inspiration came –

> *'If any one of you is without sin, let him be the first to throw a stone at her'* John 8:7 NIV

Elsewhere he describes the same process thus:

> *'I judge nothing of myself, but as I hear I judge, and my judgment is always right'* John 5:30 ASB

Creative ideas or concepts may fall into any of the following categories:

(a) Ways of developing what already exists to its maximum capacity so that the present limits of productivity or effectiveness are surpassed.

(b) Ways of adapting or modifying what exists to achieve new or improved purposes.

(c) Achieving the same end as before but doing it more simply, more economically or more profitably.

(d) Unearthing hidden, undeveloped, or hitherto unnoticed potential in people, organisations, things, situations, ideas or processes.

(e) Exploiting openings or entrepreneurial opportunities that no one else has seen.

(f) Finding answers to previously insoluble problems or new ways around difficulties or obstacles.

(g) Conceiving ideas that are innovative or completely original in the sense that they have never been done before.

6. Beyond the level of human ability there is also, for the Christian leader, access to divine wisdom.

> *'If any of you lacks wisdom, he should ask God, who gives generously to all without finding fault, and it will be given to him'*
> James 1:5 NIV

Divine wisdom does what human wisdom cannot do, it takes account of ultimate issues, ultimate consequences and ultimate values and it can guide us to decisions that will in the end produce the very best results, regardless of what the position may appear to be in the short run. Sometimes, Paul warns us, divine wisdom may be so superior to human wisdom as to appear foolishness to our limited human perspective (1 Corinthians 1:25)

Access to divine wisdom is of course never a substitute for human effort. In fact, doing the very best we can with the human resources that God has given us is often a necessary prerequisite to receiving the illumination that supercedes ordinary wisdom or commonsense. We are supposed to do our homework and then bring it to God for correction.

7. Inspiration may be a crisis or a process. Insight may come as a sudden flash of illumination or it may emerge gradually as the result of thought, discussion, tentative conclusions and modifications that come through reflection and reconsideration.

How to Develop Foresight

Many leaders reading this book, or others who are not in leadership but aspire to such responsibilities will recognise that they have functioned either intuitively or instinctively on at least some occasions in at least some of the ways we have mentioned. But as with any skill or ability, real expertise is developed only when we take what we have been doing instinctively, learn deliberately and intentionally to do it better and practice it persistently until we do it habitually. The process can be conveniently analysed into the following steps or stages.

(a) Identify your capacities or strengths,
(b) Analyse whether you are neglecting them, misusing them or making only partial use of them,
(c) Learn the correct or most effective ways to use or develop the capacities, and
(d) Endeavour to improve your skill, increase your capacities and better your results with every performance.

It needs to be emphasised that in all that we are describing we are not implying or suggesting that leaders are superior to anybody else, merely that to fulfil the role requires the use of certain largely innate capabilities. Nor are we saying that these capabilities make leaders more gifted, more intelligent, more admirable or more valuable than anyone else. We are merely saying that their role requires certain specific and essential abilities that are different from those needed for other roles. Henry Ford put it succinctly when he said, 'Asking who should be the leader is like asking who should sing tenor in the quartet.' The one with the tenor voice of course.

Chapter 2

Goals – The Leader's Aim

We come back to consider the question of goals in more detail. We have seen that a leader has to be a visionary, but he has to be more than a visionary. He has to have foresight, but even foresight is not enough unless the future is translated into specific goals and objectives. But for vision to be translated into goals it has to be conceptualised. What does that mean?

The abilities or talents that are needed in an organisation are sometimes divided into those that are operational and those that are conceptual.

Operational talents or capacities are those that are used to carry the organisation towards its objectives on a day to day basis, and to deal effectively with the issues that arise in the process. They are the abilities and strengths that are essential in management and administration, such as interpersonal skills, experience, judgment, perseverence, analytical and problem solving skills and moral integrity.

Conceptual talents on the other hand, are those that deal with the overview or the big picture, that determines the overarching or ultimate long term goal or direction of the enterprise. In conceptualising we move towards a perspective from which isolated facts, impressions, principles and insights are resolved into an imaginative whole. Conceptualising is the ability to take scattered and sometimes apparently contradictory ideas, phenomena or opinions and build them into a mental image in which each element has a logical and integral relationship with the whole. Leadership depends more on conceptual talents than operational talents.

Conceptual ability is critical for leaders in a number of areas:

1. To enable them to take the unstructured and formless potentials they see in the future and crystallise them into specific goals.
2. To anticipate contingencies and other eventualities a long way ahead and be ready to deal with them.
3. To evaluate progress and decide whether goals are likely to be attained or whether the goals themselves have to be revised or adjusted.

Getting the Right Goals

In considering the question of goals it is important for leaders to understand that it is not just any goal that will do, nor any goal that is compelling or exciting or appealing to the leaders. It is not merely a matter of getting the goals right, it is also getting the right goals, that is, goals that are:

1. right for the organisation, and
2. right for the time.

For that to be so, there has to be a certain congruence or compatability or resonance between the goals that are chosen and the aspirations or desires or motivations of the people. If the goal does not strike a chord in the hearts of the people, they simply will not follow, and leaders without followers cease to be leaders.

That is why you will sometimes find a very gifted and able leader with a truly charismatic personality and an admirable and worthy vision, driven to despair and often bitterness because nobody will rally to his call. People admire and even applaud his vision and wish him well but nobody is willing to commit themselves to be a part of it. Worse still, along comes some raw and untried would-be leader with a much less dazzling vision and far less persuasive power, and suddenly everybody wants to buy into it or help to bring it to pass. What was missing in the first case and present in the second was resonance between the goals and the people.

Successful politicians have this capacity to a marked degree. They are somehow able to sense the 'hot' issues or timely subjects that are likely to catch the mood or interest of the public. Their less successful colleagues are meanwhile pontificating about other more worthy causes and merely irritating or boring the electorate.

Staying in Touch

The factors involved in this capacity are not easy to pin down but one thing they do point out is that leaders not only have to be out in front of the people, they also have to stay in touch with the people. If leaders get too far out in front, the people will lose touch with them, and even more important, they will lose touch with the people. Leaders in other words have to be reaching out to worthwhile objectives but they have always to hold those goals in one hand and their people in the other hand so that they can judge or evaluate the likely compatibility or resonance between them.

The leaders who do it best are those who have developed an on-going flow of both formal and informal two-way communication between them and their people. They are always talking with their people and they are always listening to their people. We say that they 'have an ear to the ground'. In this way they are constantly building up in their minds a bank of impressions, opinions, ideas, thoughts, feelings and perceptions that gives them an intuitive but accurate sense of where their people are at and what will, or will not stir them into action and commitment.

In a way that they might not even be able to explain, such leaders will know and will tell you, 'That would go down like a lead balloon with our people' or 'We are not quite ready for something like that yet, but give us another six months and our folk would go for that,' or 'Our people would really buy into that in a big way.'

The characteristics of the relationship between leaders and people that make such judgments possible can be helpfully clarified by examining both what it is and what it is not.

1. Firstly, it is not eavesdropping by the leaders or merely their plugging into the grapevine or the informal communication network in the organisation. Leaders who try to do that create an anxious atmosphere every time they appear on the scene; they are felt to be 'snooping' or 'quizzing' people and the common question after they have gone is 'I wonder what he was after that time?'

2. Secondly it springs always out of a genuine interest on the part of the leaders in their people and an honest desire to get to know them as persons. The good shepherd, Jesus points out *'calls his sheep by name'* (John 10:3), that is he knows their characteristics and their temperaments and their individual identities. The interest must however be genuine, it cannot be successfully put on or pretended. People soon spot a phony.

3. Thirdly there has to be an atmosphere of trust between people and leaders so that people feel safe enough to say real things to the leaders and not just the things that are expected of them. In other words, people have to be sure that their leaders:

(a) Really want to know what they think
(b) Will treat their opinions with respect, and
(c) Will not hold it against them if they do not agree with the leaders' views

4. Fourthly, sharing must be mutual, that is leaders have to share their dreams, aspirations, hopes and visions with the people.

Leaders obviously have to be wise about how much detail they disclose as far as specific visions and goals are concerned because there are dangers in the premature disclosure of matters that are under serious consideration, and we will deal with this later. But the free flowing give-and-take of informal discussion provides the opportunity for ideas and opinions to be exchanged, hypothetical cases to be floated and considered and continuous soundings to be taken of where people are at in their thinking and their aspirations.

Goals and the Time Scale

Goals are commonly classified in terms of the time scale involved, that is, how far their completion is in the future and therefore the length of time that we will have to commit resources in order to achieve them. Goals are therefore usually divided into those that are:

1. Long term – say 5 to 15 or more years ahead
2. Medium term – generally 2 to 5 years, and
3. Short term – weekly, monthly, quarterly etc.

Regardless of the specific time frames, long term goals must be settled first. Medium and short term goals must be compatible with the long term goals and are judged by whether they advance the long term objective.

Height and Distance

In considering goals, leaders also face inescapable tensions over the questions of height and distance, that is, how high do they aim for, and how far ahead do they set their targets. These are particularly important matters in relation to the response of the people to the goals presented to them.

1. If the goals are set too high, they may be written off in the people's minds as unreachable and unrealistic.

If the goals are set too low, they will not arouse much interest or enthusiasm.

2. If the goals are too far distant, it may be hard to get immediate participation, because

(a) There seems to be plenty of time and no need to do anything straight away, or

(b)   The thought of putting effort in now when the pay-off is so far away is not particularly rewarding.

On the other hand, if the goals are too near at hand enthusiasm will be short lived because they are soon attained.

The Long Term Goal

There is a case for dividing long term goals into two main classes.

1. Goals that are quite specific and quite limited in scope but that are of necessity going to take a long time to accomplish. An example could be the objective to build a new church complex, where it is going to take some years to gather the finances and even then the complete project will have to be built in stages over a further number of years.

2. Overarching goals that determine the purpose and direction of the organisation for a long time ahead. These are the true long term objectives, and they have the following characteristics:

(a)   The longer the time span, the more general and the less specific they will be. For example, Abraham's long term goal, given to him by God, was very imprecise;

> *'Leave your country, your people, and your father's household and go to the land I will show you.'*   Genesis 12:1

Only when Abraham is moving towards the goal do the identity, the dimensions and the boundaries of the land become gradually revealed. (Genesis 13:14–17, 15:17–21)

(b)   Nevertheless, the goals must be clear enough and compelling enough to keep the organisation on course in bad times as well as in good. In bad times it can take all the pull exerted by a powerful goal to get the organisation through.

(c)   They must also be powerful enough to override short term distractions, that is, attractive short term opportunities,

25

good in themselves, but that would in the long run be diversions from the real long term objective.

(d) While long term goals should be clear, they should not be closed. The most enduring goals are those that can always be added to without losing their distinctiveness or their attraction. The great prophetic goal of the Promise, beginning with Abraham, and added to by Moses, David and the prophets, is an example of this. The prophetic future is clear but always open ended, with room for God to take us by surprise and leading to unimaginable openness of the age to come.

The Mission Statement

Long term or overarching objectives often take the form of a mission statement that may be written into the constitution of the church or the founding instrument of a corporation or organisation. One of the shortest, but best examples of recent times is the mission statement of Youth With a Mission – 'TO KNOW GOD AND TO MAKE GOD KNOWN.' That provides an open but quite clear and precise long term objective against which any and all of the proposed activities can be judged as to their legitimacy within the mission.

When the church to which I belong was beginning, much to our surprise, to emerge as a congregation we spent a considerable time on this issue. Eventually we drew up a list of what we considered were the long term objectives of that particular Christian community. We divided them into objectives for our personal lives, objectives for our corporate life and objectives for our mission. (See Appendix A) A large sized reproduction of the final statement was framed and hung in the entrance foyer of the church building.

With the benefit and hindsight of 17 year's experience I would not change any of those statements. Their presence and particularly the fact that they have been publicly displayed have been of inestimable value to the leadership over the years. At any time, people could point to one or other of the objectives and ask, 'What are we doing to fulfil this?' or point to any of the activities that the church was involved in and ask, 'Where and how does this fit in with our overall objectives?'

What surprises me now is how few churches have such long term objectives or mission statements, or if there is one it is hidden in the archives or in a constitution or confession of faith to which nobody ever refers or has access to.

Clarifying Goals

Goals, particularly the long term and the medium term ones emerge out of two different types of thinking.

1. First there is creative thinking that generates possibilities. We have dealt with that to some extent already.

2. Second there is judgmental thinking that evaluates possibilities in terms of their practicality, their merit and their likely outcomes.

In practice the two types of thinking are always to some extent integrated and carried on more or less simultaneously. They are not to be kept in two watertight compartments. Thus the process of evaluating possibilities may itself suggest modifications or adaptations to a proposal or may generate new or innovative alternatives.

The aim of this type of judgmental thinking is not only to get the goals right but to get them clear. Unless leaders are crystal clear about the goals they have chosen they will never be able to make themselves clear to the people. In fact the process of communication always results in some loss of clarity so that if leaders are unclear to begin with, what they communicate to their people will be even more confused.

Note also that evaluation is not one single uniform process. Different people have different ways of examining things so as to arrive at a conclusion about their worth or significance or implications. One of the strengths of team leadership, an eldership for example, is that members of the team will probably tackle the process of evaluation from several different perspectives so that a proposal has to pass a fairly searching scrutiny to gain approval.

Here are some of the likely perspectives:

1. The Analyst
This is the person who always breaks a thing down into its constituent parts, considers the characteristics of each and finds out how the parts relate to the whole. He takes complex ideas apart as precisely as he takes an intricate mechanism to pieces.

2. The Assessor
Value, merit, worth, importance and significance are the categories in which this person customarily thinks. Sometimes the conclusions are arrived at as the result of a quick once-over, at other times they are reached after the methodical application of specific criteria. Practicality, quality, authenticity and cost effectiveness are the assessor's main interests.

3. The Calculator
This is the person who likes to work towards exact quantitative or predictive determinations, therefore he thinks in terms of budget projections, cost estimates or quantifiable results. He wants to see figures not just vague ideas.

4. The Monitor
The monitor usually focuses on how things measure up to recognised standards or established criteria. A proposal will therefore be evaluated in relation to previous decisions or precedents or the way in which it harmonises with, or deviates from the policies that have already been set or those set by other relevant authorities.

5. The Intuitive
This person's evaluative capacity is characterised by intuitive insight and shrewd discernment. He or she has the ability to see through appearances, to stand in the other person's shoes, to discern their needs, problems and expectations and to anticipate what they are likely to do. In situations where people

interests predominate, or where there is the need for the kind of discernment that leads to effective strategising in dealing with others, the intuitive person shines.

6. The Judge

This person is motivated to make decisions or choices based on an even handed weighing up of the pros and cons of a course of action or a rational examination of the relative merits of alternative policies. Once all the pertinent information or views have been laid out, he or she reviews them and sorts them out in accordance with their strong and weak points. In other words the judge is the person who generally brings the discussion to a head and insists that some decision be made.

Chapter 3

The Question of Timing

The question of timing is another critical area for leaders because they have the responsibility of deciding, not only what is to be done but also when to begin to implement the decision. Deciding the right time to move is also part of the responsibility of the shepherd:

> 'When *he has brought out all his own he goes on ahead of them and his sheep follow him because they know his voice.'*
> John 10:4 NIV

Leaders, we have seen, are always oriented towards the future and therefore in one sense they are always reaching out into the unknown and the 'not here yet'. But the leader operates in a totally different time frame to the visionary.

The visionary or the dreamer lives almost entirely in the future, he dreams his dreams or she paints her visions of what could be, but neither of them have to do anything to actualise their pictures.

The leader on the other hand has to operate on the boundary line between the future and the present, that is to say, he or she has to take the critical decisions that will draw the future into the present, that will attempt to actualise the vision and will commit resources and manpower to the task of concretising the dream.

That is the leader's unique and daunting territory. People who are not leaders do not understand it or shun it as risky, uncertain and stressful but to leaders it is the 'cutting edge', the place where the really exciting business takes place.

In the church this difference is the reason for the commonly experienced tension between prophets and elders. The prophetic word, when it is a genuine prophetic word comes to the prophet out of eternity and therefore it has an immediacy and a timelessness about it that makes it difficult for us to fit it into our space-time continuum. The prophet, of course, cannot do other than give the message word for word as he receives it, therefore he looks for instant and immediate obedience to the word that always has the impact of 'Now!'

But the responsibility of deciding the 'when' to which the word applies is not the responsibility of the prophet but that of the elders, it is something they have to wrestle with before the Lord. The prophet often finds that hard to live with; to him, if the word is not obeyed by tomorrow afternoon, or the end of the week at the latest, judgment will be on its way. But the elders cannot delegate their responsibility for the timing of the word to the prophet, any more than he can delegate his responsibility to them.

Deciding the Time

The specific factors to be taken into account in deciding when it is the right time to act will obviously vary from one situation to another. Nevertheless the common issues that are likely to be involved will generally include the following:

1. There is usually a time, which may be long or short, when the final decision has to be held in abeyance until the leaders have secured enough information, or reached sufficient clarity to enable them to decide.

This stage will involve gathering information and analysing data, making forecasts and estimates and probably a lot of discussion and prayer. It may also involve floating numbers of alternative scenarios or hypothetical models, or taking exploratory or tentative steps from which it is still possible to draw back. But the leaders know clearly that they are not yet at the place where they can make a final and irrevocable decision to commit themselves to the project or to abandon it altogether.

2. During this stage leaders will often face pressure from those who want an early decision or who cannot understand why the leaders are still 'dithering around' or don't seem able to make up their mind. There may also be pressure from circumstances that clamour for action to be taken.

It can be a severe test of the leaders' capacity, and their character to refuse to submit to external pressure when they know full well that they do not have enough data or enough understanding to enable them to make a good decision. But to surrender to such external pressure can mean that effective control of the decision making situation has actually slipped out of their hands.

3. Nevertheless there comes a point in time when a decision has to be made, and leaders have to be willing to take the plunge with less than the degree of certainty they would like to have. The tension that leaders always face at this point is:

(a) If they move too soon, later information coming in may show that they have made a mistake, but

(b) If they wait until they have all the information they would like to have they will almost certainly be too late.

The ability to get the time right is one of the marks of the good leader. The way they do it is less clear. Probably it has to do both with the gathering of data, impressions, cues and hints from the wider than usual span of awareness we discussed when dealing with foresight, the intuitive kind of hunch that comes from discernment and the wisdom that comes from experience.

Jumping the Information Gap

Two of the essential characteristics that separate leaders from those who are not leaders, and good leaders from poor leaders, come into play at this stage. They are the ability and the willingness to:

1. Leap the information gap, that is, make a decision on the less than perfect information they have and what they can predict or project about the proposal or the situation, and

2. Step out into the relatively unknown and uncertain future with the inner confidence that when they face the questions and hazards that will arise, and about which they can hardly guess at this stage, they will nevertheless find within themselves the ability and creative insights to find the right answers and make the right decisions.

This is always a faith step, in that leaders are trusting their judgment or what they perceive as being the leading or wisdom imparted by the Holy Spirit, and because it is a faith step it never becomes easy. It is something that those who are not leaders find difficult to understand or find stressful and anxiety creating if they are involved in making such decisions.

Judged from outside leadership it sometimes appears more daring than it actually is because people do not have access to all the information that may be available to the leaders or they do not see the future as clearly as the leaders do. On occasions it seems to them utterly reckless and presumptuous, at other times so easy that anybody could do it. Both conclusions are wrong.

On the other hand, leaders have to be aware of what they are doing, that is, when making decisions they need to distinguish very clearly between:

1. Hard data that represents facts they can be sure of,
2. Estimates and forecasts that represent probabilities or educated guesses, and
3. The place where there is an information gap that has to be bridged.

If they are not aware of where the information gap is, they will often make a poor decision, doing the wrong thing at the right time or doing the right thing at the wrong time.

Leaders often operate in this way intuitively or instinctively, we 'fly by the seat of our pants'. Sometimes we make really good decisions although we cannot explain the steps by which we arrived at them. Even when we do something naturally, we rarely become consistently good at it unless we learn to do it deliberately and seek to improve our performance every time.

That means that the question of timing needs to be consciously addressed along with all the other factors that are involved in the decision making process. Sometimes timing is an obviously critical factor, on other occasions it may be relatively unimportant or of low level priority. These latter occasions are opportunities to improve our ability to size up the implications of the time factor at little risk so that we are more skilful and more confident about addressing the issue when it is of graver importance.

Chapter 4

Imparting the Vision

It is not enough to get a vision, or even to conceptualise it into clear and well defined goals. If you cannot get people to follow you towards those goals you are not a leader. I remember a young man coming to me one time in the depths of discouragement and angry despair. He had a vision for a particular form of ministry and he had the vision articulated clearly in a document of several pages. He had been promoting his vision for nearly a year trying to get key people interested but nothing ever got together. What, he wanted to know, was the matter with people in the church? They had no sense of commitment and no willingness to get involved in his mission.

I had eventually to point out to him that the hard reality was that very likely he was just not a leader. People do not generally follow visions or dreams or schemes or ideas, they follow leaders. Therefore leaders, even if they have the right goals, that make contact with the aspirations of the people, need something more. They also have to be effective persuaders and relationship builders. And the way in which they present the vision and the goal has a good deal to do with the way in which people receive them and respond to them. Therefore the presentation requires serious consideration, it is not merely window dressing.

The Aim of the Presentation

The goal that the leaders have accepted for themselves has now to be presented and expressed in a way that will give direction and a sense of certainty to the people. That means that:

1. It must give a specific direction that people can recognise and identify, not merely a range of optional or possible directions.

2. People must have confidence that the direction or goal that is presented is not going to change or be altered unexpectedly. If goals or directions are changed drastically during the stage of imparting a vision it is often fatal to the whole vision and generally an indication that the presentation was premature.

3. It must excite the imagination of the people. This depends largely on the extent to which the leaders themselves are genuinely excited by the vision. If their imagination is not fired, they will never ignite others. What has to take place is that the future that only the leaders have seen heretofore is now brought within range so that others can see it and be captured by it.

4. It must challenge people to participate. The presentation must do more than rouse people's appreciation or admiration, or even convince them of the likelihood that the project could succeed. It must confront them with a challenge for their personal involvement to help make it happen. If it does not do this, the best presentation in the world has missed the mark. Yet it is often here that the nerve of the leaders fail them, they hesitate to press for a commitment in case it is not forthcoming.

5. There is also a special challenge faced by leaders on some occasions when they have to present an objective or goal and try to gain a response even though the ultimate goal has to be held back meantime because it cannot yet be understood or appreciated.

Steps in Imparting the Vision

1. The first necessity is that the leaders have let the vision grow within them. They need to dwell on it, feed on it, live on it,

dream it. It has to become in them what, in a different context altogether, the word of the Lord became in Jeremiah,

> *'His word is in my heart like a fire,*
> *a fire shut up in my bones.*
> *I am weary of holding it in;*
> *indeed, I cannot.'*
> Jeremiah 20:9b NIV

When the vision gets to that stage, it is probably the right time to begin to impart it.

2. It is important to avoid premature disclosure. There is abiding significance in the Biblical phrase 'When the time had fully come – '. In other words, there is a stage when it is too soon to be presenting goals. This is not secrecy, it is merely allowing time for objectives and concepts to be refined and clarified and for uncertainties to be removed or reduced.

If goals and visions are shared too soon, people may respond to something only to find that it is later abandoned or drastically revised, or their response may be negative simply because the case has been inadequately prepared and many of their questions cannot yet be answered.

This does not mean that leaders are not to take people into their confidence as to the general directions they are looking at, nor that there is not valuable input to be obtained from many people along the way. But it means that leaders need wisdom as to when they should go public with their final plans.

3. Before a vision or goal can be adequately and effectively presented, the leaders must have the conviction and confidence to have decided beforehand that, given a favourable response by the people they will go for it with all their hearts. Few things erode confidence more than for people to have a goal presented to them, and to say Yes! to it, but then find the leaders hesitating or having second thoughts.

4. The presentation must be prepared thoroughly. That means gathering and organising all the material and information on which the leaders have based their decisions. Often it is valuable to have available the records of the stages through

which the deliberations have gone. Many of the questions that will be raised will have already been considered at depth and it is reassuring to have access to that evidence rather than relying on memory.

5. In the presentation of the evidence on which the case rests, leaders must be very open and honest about:

(a) How much consists of hard data and solid fact,
(b) How much consists of estimates or approximations or forecasts,
(c) What are the faith steps, that is, the places where 'bridging the information gap' has taken place,
(d) Where the leaders consider that they are moving on direct guidance or a word from the Lord.

The validity of all four types of data or input, including (d) must be open to be questioned, discussed and validated.

Leaders must be very conscientious and careful about this aspect. If they give the impression that there are certainties where there are, in fact, faith steps, then people who discover that later, may feel they have been deceived, moreover their faith has not been operative at the very point where it is required.

6. Equal frankness and honesty are required in making clear the costs, sacrifices and risks that are involved in the venture, and the obstacles and difficulties that may be encountered. It is useful to remember in this regard that alongside man's created need for certainty and security there is an equally created need for uncertainty and for risk. We have a need to be challenged and tested and called to put our abilities on the line in the face of daunting circumstances. Our need for security is met by a God who is always the same, *'I the Lord do not change.'* (Malachi 3:6 NIV) Our need for uncertainty is met by a God who is always doing new things. *'Forget the former things; do not dwell on the past. See I am doing a new thing!'* (Isaiah 43:18–19 NIV)

People do not mind accepting risks as long as they are doing it with their eyes open.

7. Leaders must also deal fairly and honestly with questions

and objections that are raised. Regardless of the terms in which these may be couched, the basic reasons behind them have to be discovered.

(a) Is it because the leaders have not been clear enough in their presentation or explanations? Do not expect people to get in one meeting, or one hearing to the level of understanding that it took the leaders six months to reach.

(b) Is it hesitancy over the cost of commitment, or are people struggling with the faith leap? If so, be understanding about their position. You may need to give them time to think it through or go back over the ground again.

(c) Is it prophetic, that is, are the objections a check from the Holy Spirit to which we need to give attention even at this late stage?

(d) Or is it a question of principle or conscience as far as the particular person is concerned? Here also we need to be very careful and very understanding if we are asking somebody to forego a question of personal principle for the sake of group consensus.

8. To guard against overlooking things that need to be seriously considered we need to ensure that at every stage of the proceedings any negative viewpoint is fairly and adequately presented. Most times you will find that all the objectors are really after is assurance that the leaders have considered those negatives and with full awareness of them have nevertheless decided to go ahead.

9. Along with the faith steps and the sacrifices that may be involved, leaders must affirm the possibilities. They have to communicate confidence in the outcome, a conviction that the difficulties, whatever they may be, are surmountable, and the goal however distant it may seem, is reachable. In the ultimate, no matter how convincing the facts of the case may be, the leaders have to dig down inside themselves and find the faith to inspire those they are trying to enlist. Evidence helps to convince people, but only faith will move them, and the task of leaders is to provide that faith. Many, many times in the course

of the journey towards the goal they will have to dig down to find the faith and the courage that are needed, therefore they had better learn how to do it at the very beginning. If they don't, it is predictable that there never will be a serious beginning to the project.

10. But leaders have to go further than merely stirring faith in people that the goal is reachable or creating in them the desire to be a part of it. Leaders have to plant the vision in the people's hearts so that they 'buy into' it. That rarely happens straight away. People begin with a commitment to participate, but the commitment may initially be quite tentative, or be to some extent an impulsive response that the person on reflection hesitates over. The leaders' motivational job is never accomplished until the people begin to 'own' the vision for themselves, and that is what must always be aimed for.

11. Thereafter leaders must work at building an identification between themselves and their people in relation to the goal so that to the people it becomes not the leaders' goal but their own. It is only when the goal becomes corporately owned that it can survive the death or departure of the leader or leaders who called it into being in the first place. Many of the problems with succession or the difficulties that occur when there are changes in leadership arise because this point has been overlooked. When new leaders take over, it is found too late that they have a different vision or different goals or cannot identify with what is already going on.

Sometimes leaders resist letting go of the vision so that it can become corporately owned. They want to retain a proprietary stake in it, because they had the vision before anybody else did, and therefore they want it always to be identified with them personally. They eventually discover that if you do that, the same thing happens to the vision as Jesus said would happen to those who try to save their life – they lose it.

12. Finally, remember that the motivational task is never done once for all. An essential part of the function of leaders is to continually reiterate, reinforce, clarify and redefine goals along the way. In difficult times the vision tends to fade and

enthusiasm needs to be rekindled; in changed circumstances goals may need to be restated differently; in the light of experience they may have to be revised, or modified. A course on a map may be a straight line drawn with a ruler, but actual travel on the ground is never like that, it is rather a continual series of stops and starts and short scale course adjustments around obstacles. The presentation is a route map of the direction to be taken but actual progress towards organisational goals requires constant navigational corrections.

Chapter 5

Danger – Power at Work

All leaders handle power. In a sense, power goes with the job. Leaders are the ones with the power to determine what is to be done and how it is to be done. They decide when it is to be done and who is to do it.

Leaders are also positioned at the centre of the communication network in the organisation, therefore they have more and better information than most people as to what is going on. Here, as elsewhere, knowledge is power.

Power is exhilarating stuff to handle, even on a small scale. It is ego boosting. The team captain decides on the plays or the field settings and a dozen other adults jump to do his bidding. A prime minister or a president makes a decision and overnight millions of people including the most powerful in the land have to comply whether they like it or not.

It is the same with knowledge. Knowledge puffs up, says Paul (1 Corinthians 8:1). It feeds our feelings of self importance to know things that other people don't know and to be able to make decisions on the basis of inside knowledge.

But power is as dangerous as unstable dynamite, not only to those it is used on but to those who exercise it. Lord Acton the British statesman is remembered for his famous dictum, 'All power corrupts and absolute power corrupts absolutely.' History is littered with the sad evidence that proves the correctness of his judgment, the wreckage of good men and good women who began with the best of intentions but were corrupted and destroyed by the power they wielded. And it happens inside the church as frequently and as painfully as it happens in the world.

Is Power Corrupt?

Why has this so often been the case? Some would say that power itself is fallen and corrupt and has been so ever since the primal sin of Lucifer. The essence and the expression of his rebellion was the illegitimate reaching for power and authority that was not his right to possess.

> 'You said in your heart
> "I will ascend to heaven,
> I will raise my throne above the stars of God;
> I will sit enthroned on the mount of assembly,
> On the utmost heights of the sacred mountain.
> I will ascend above the tops of the clouds;
> I will make myself like the Most High."'
>
> Isaiah 14:13–14 NIV

If that is the case, it should come as no surprise to find that the fall of mankind also brings power struggles into human relationships. The created partnership of equals between man and woman is replaced by domination on the one side and manipulation on the other (Genesis 3:16) and the first confrontations between men end in murder and violence.

> 'And when they were in the field, Cain rose up against his brother Abel and killed him'
>
> Genesis 4:8 RSV

> 'And Lamech said to his wives,
> "Ada and Zillah
> Hear my voice you wives of Lamech,
> hearken to what I say:
> I have slain a man for wounding me
> a young man for striking me."'
>
> Genesis 4:23 RSV

From the very beginning power makes it clear that it does not live happily with rivals or opponents.

Furthermore when man begins to build his cities, the city itself becomes a power, drawing to itself the power of population, of military might, of money and of occultism. Beginning with Babel the city becomes the enduring symbol for man's corporate lust for power.

God says,

> *'I am God, and there is no other;*
> *I am God, and there is none like me.'*   Isaiah 46:9 NIV

Babylon the archetypal city, the fallen power, says,

> *'I am, and there is none besides me.*
> *I will never be a widow*
> *Or suffer the loss of children'*   Isaiah 47:8 NIV

And in the spiritual realm the demonic powers dominate the world system and oppress the whole of the human race. (Ephesians 6:12)

If power itself is fallen and corrupt it is no wonder that its use has such devastating effects. The sad fact is that historically, power handled by the church has often been as corrupt, as evil and as shamefully tyrannical in its outworkings as that wielded by any dictator.

Is Power Morally Neutral?

On the other hand there are those who would say that it is not power as such that is corrupt, but the power users. Power, like wealth or nuclear energy or printing is morally neutral, it is what is done with it that is either good or bad. God, it is pointed out, has all power but he is never in danger of being corrupted by his omnipotence. And even in a fallen world and in the hands of fallen men and women, power brings blessing as well as curse, it saves and benefits life as well as endangering or destroying it. In fact we cannot turn the argument round and praise powerlessness because it also can be a bane and a curse for those trapped in it.

Corrupting Effects of Power

But even if power is morally neutral, we still have to ask what it is in people's fallen nature that makes them peculiarly susceptible to the baneful effects of power when they have it in their hands to use for too long. When we ask these questions we discover that the Bible, which knows far more than Lord Acton about the dangers of power, gives a comprehensive analysis of the evil effects it can have on the characters of those who handle it. Every leader should study this section very carefully, as I do even as I write it, because the onset of power disintegration is very gradual and very insidious and the early symptoms appear very innocuous. In fact a reluctance to face the possibility that we ourselves can be adversely affected by handling power may well mean that we have already been influenced.

Here are the classic symptoms of a character that is beginning to show the corrupting effects of using or handling power.

1. Pride
The evil of pride is that it gives us an exaggerated sense of our own importance or significance compared with other people. Pride is not necessarily the heart condition of the person who is conspicuous or to whom others look up; it is the attitude of the person who, regardless of the position they occupy, looks down on others, secure in their own superiority and self-conceit.

> '*We have heard of Moab's pride –*
> *her overweening pride and conceit,*
> *her pride and arrogance and the haughtiness of her heart.*'
> Jeremiah 48:29 NIV

Leaders are particularly susceptible to the sin of pride, firstly because of the intoxicating effects of wielding power over other people. Personal vanity feeds on the ability to do or command things that the mass of people cannot do.

Secondly they are continually at risk because of the deference that is shown to them by other people. All the terminology of leadership subtly reinforces this attitude. Leaders are 'over' others and others are 'under' the leaders; leaders are the 'superiors' and the followers are the 'subordinates'. Leaders are 'promoted' to positions of authority, and each time they are promoted they go 'higher' up the ladder.

Thirdly, pride is itself a fallen form of confidence, and confidence, including self confidence is a necessary attribute of leadership. The uncertain, and indecisive leader who lacks confidence is a danger to the whole organisation. But it is not easy to prevent a legitimate self confidence from sliding over into pride. Here are some of the danger signals to watch for.

(a) The give-away of pride is the effect it has on our view of other people and on our attitudes towards them. The attitude of pride is that if I am to be better, then the others have to be worse; if I am to be valuable, then the others have to be worthless; if I am to be superior, then the others are necessarily inferior.

(b) Pride differs from the drive to win against competition or even the desire to come out on top or be the best. Competitive success requires that my opponents are worthy antagonists otherwise the achievement in beating them has no merit. Pride on the other hand despises opponents or competitors as being beneath my notice.

(c) Pride is one of the sins that comes out of man's fallen heart. From despising other men it goes on to despise God, it becomes what the Greeks called 'hubris' – impious pride.

> *'The beginning of man's pride is to depart from the lord, his heart has forsaken his Maker.'*
>
> Ecclesiasticus 10:12 (Apocrypha)

Therefore, pride always merits the strongest judgment from God.

> *'Everyone who is proud in heart is an abomination to the Lord.*
> *Pride goes before destruction and a haughty spirit before a fall.'*
> Proverbs 16:5, 18 AV

2. Arrogance

Power leads inevitably to arrogance. Proverbs joins them together, *'pride, arrogance and the evil way and the perverse mouth.'* (Proverbs 8:13 NKJV) Arrogance often shows up in leaders as the unwillingness to be checked or opposed or questioned in any way. It has been called 'the wrongness of those who think they are always right.'

Our very success as leaders in the decisions we have made, particularly in the times when we have been shown to be right in the face of opposition or contrary opinion can subtly seduce us into an arrogant disregard of other people's viewpoints, or an impatience in answering questions or resentment when our will is opposed. We feel we know best, we do not need advice and second opinions we can do without.

Any over-sensitivity or defensiveness in facing questions or handling criticism, and any rancour at being opposed need to be watched very carefully because it can be interpreted as arrogance or indeed a sign of it taking root in our heart.

The greatest danger of arrogance however, is not only the damage it can do to our relationships, but the deception to which it can so easily lead.

> *'The pride of your heart has deceived you,*
> *You who live in the clefts of the rocks*
> *Who say to yourself,*
> *"Who can bring me down to the ground?"'*   Obadiah 3 NIV

Without the acid of objective questioning to keep us in touch with reality, we can be led astray by distorted perceptions, grandiose delusions, poor judgment or faulty discernment. But it is just such critical examination that arrogance resents most bitterly and rejects most indignantly.

The more successful we are as leaders, the more we need our critics, even when they are wrong, because at the very least they help to save us from the dangers of arrogance. We also desperately need those who care enough for us to 'bring us down to earth' when they suspect that we are in danger of becoming inflated with our success and ballooning with our own vanity and self importance.

3. Self Aggrandisement

Another seduction to which power users such as leaders can easily succumb is using power and the things to which power gives them access, for their own personal ends. Sooner or later it includes using people to achieve the same selfish ends. The ends may take the form of monetary or material gain, as witness the obscene opulence of some leaders of impoverished nations, or the aim may be the achievement of position or status, or it may be the adulation and prestige that go with the position. Whatever the specific ends may be they have one thing in common, they are for the leaders' self gratification.

> 'This is what the Sovereign Lord says: "Woe to the shepherds of Israel who only take care of themselves! Should not shepherds take care of the flock? You eat the curds, clothe yourself with the wool, and slaughter the choice animals but you do not take care of the flock."'

> 'This is what the Sovereign Lord says: "I am against the shepherds and will hold them accountable for my flock."'
>
> Ezekiel 34:2, 10 NIV

Self aggrandisement is particularly blameworthy in leaders because they are exploiting the particular advantages that their position gives them for self centred purposes and thereby betraying the trust that people have placed in them. Implicit in the attitude that makes this possible is contempt for the people, seeing them as merely exploitable or expendable means that can be used to achieve whatever ends the leaders find useful.

4. Insensitivity

For the sake of the task in hand, leaders often have to insist on people doing things they don't particularly want to do or in ways they don't like or at times that inconvenience them. But this power can also make leaders very thoughtless and insensitive towards the people who are under their authority. They tend to ride roughshod over their rights and have little compunction about hurting their feelings. Leaders' very absorption with their goals and the success that rides on reaching the goals can sometimes make them quite oblivious to the effects on the people who are helping them to reach their goals. They inconvenience people, make demands on their time, replace them at short notice and generally act in arbitrary or high handed ways.

There is a classic example of this kind of insensitivity when Reheboam succeeded his father Solomon to the throne of Israel. At the very beginning of his reign he faced a deputation from the northern tribes, seeking relief from the tax burden under which they laboured. The elders who had served with Solomon advised the young king:

> *'Today if you will be a servant to these people and serve them and give them a favourable answer, they will always be your servants.'*　　　1 Kings 12:7 NIV

But Reheboam followed instead the advice of his peers, the young power hungry elite who had grown up with him. He answered the deputation thus:

> *'My father made your yoke heavy; I will make it even heavier. My father scourged you with whips, I will scourge you with scorpions.'*　　　1 Kings 12:14 NIV

This gross moral insensibility lost Reheboam the allegiance of the ten northern tribes and destroyed forever the unity of the kingdom.

In less blatant but equally disastrous ways such as ingratitude, thoughtlessness and taking people for granted, leaders can lose the hearts of their people. People may still acknowledge the rightness and the desirability of the goals, they may struggle to remain committed but deep in their hearts they feel somehow 'used' and 'ripped off'.

5. Domination

When leaders find themselves under threat they can very easily succumb to the temptation of maintaining their position at any cost and by any means. It is not difficult to rationalise this stance, that is to find justifying reasons that are not the real ones but are more respectable than the real ones, for example, 'It is in the best interests of the organisation, and even essential for its survival that we stay at the helm' or, 'the motives of those trying to take over control are very suspect and deeply flawed' or, 'We will gladly step down and make room for younger men and women, but this is quite the wrong time to do so' – and so on.

Again this is a temptation to which leaders are particularly prone, both because of their temperament and because of the nature of their role. Leaders very often have to stand firm, to decline to be intimidated by daunting circumstances and to tough it out in the face of opposition and hostility. They are expected to conquer difficulties and prevail over strong forces that oppose the organisation or its mission.

But when these abilities are pressed into service to maintain leaders in their accustomed position regardless of the rights of others they become evil. In secular situations, military force or the power of the police or various forms of political or economic pressure or propaganda may be used to dominate the opposition or overawe possible dissent. In churches the pressure is more likely to be social or psychological or emotional. Even more reprehensible, something like divine sanction is sometimes claimed for the status quo. The leaders are 'the Lord's anointed' or the 'God-ordained shepherds' and any opposition is seen as rebellion against divinely instituted authority.

Domination can begin by simple politicking in the church

meeting, the mustering of supporters to get a project approved or an election going the way we want it to go. It can progress to the more dubious tactics of manipulating the agenda or managing the flow of business to deny the opposition the opportunity of being adequately heard, or stacking the meeting with those known to be favourably disposed to the proposal. When the gloves are off it can descend to the open railroading or discrediting of dissenters, all in the name of unity. But back of all these methods is the same prideful, ruthless drive of power to dominate and to have its way at all costs.

6. Tyranny

This is the final stage in the misuse of power where the leaders' authority is totally uncontrolled and coercive. There is no longer even the pretence of having to have good reasons for the orders given, they are to be obeyed just because they have been given, no matter how unreasonable or capricious they may be.

It is clear that the people are no longer being led any more, they are being oppressed; they have ceased to be even means to an end, they have become prey. They are captives who need to be rescued and prisoners who need to be set free.

> 'Can the prey be taken from the mighty,
> Or the captives of the tyrant be rescued?
> Surely, thus says the Lord
> "Even the captives of the mighty will be taken away,
> And the prey of the tyrant be rescued;
> or I will contend with those who contend with you,
> And I will save your children."'   Isaiah 49:24–25 RSV

Worldly Means of Controlling Power

Because of the manifest abuses and evils arising from the exercise of power, there have been continuous attempts to find ways of keeping it under control, or at least mitigating the worst effects of its misuse. The approaches to the problem fall into two main classes; sometimes both are used together.

Checks and Balances

The first solution is to divide the power up so that it is not concentrated in one person or one group or one office. Instead it is apportioned amongst several different power centres. The aim is to create a system of checks and balances so that the excessive or unjust exercise of power by one power centre can be restrained or redressed by the others. Moreover the system is intended to be a check against the accumulation of too much power in the hands of one power centre because if it attempts to increase its authority it will meet strong opposition from powerful antagonists that are sensitive to any disturbance in the status quo.

An example of a system of checks and balances is found in the political systems of most western democracies. Power is generally divided between the legislature (A House of Representatives or Parliament), the executive (Cabinet or a President) and the judiciary (the courts of law). Sometimes the division of power is enshrined in a written constitution or bill of rights, or sometimes it is part of a code of unwritten conventions that have been built up over the centuries.

In exactly the same way and for the same reasons, business corporations have their articles of association and churches have their constitutions where, amongst other things the division of power and the recognised procedures for the exercise of legitimate power are laid down.

These systems undoubtedly have value and in the political arena they provide some protection against at least the more flagrant abuses of power. They are however subject to two grave defects.

1. They often lead to a state of perpetual skirmishing at the boundaries between power centres, each of which is trying to increase its area of authority and jealously guarding against any intrusion into its preserves or any erosion of its rights.

Anyone who has been involved in moves to change the constitution of a church or the rules of an organisation will sometimes have been appalled at the politicking that goes on, the tactics that are used and the hostility and heat that is generated. They happen because what is at stake is power and power never sits easily with rivals.

Furthermore alliances between power centres to reduce or eliminate the power or rights of other power centres and then to share the spoils are by no means uncommon. Peace at the borders is therefore usually a fragile and uneasy truce.

2. Any system of checks and balances will function successfully only where there is already tacit agreement that power should be shared. It has proved to be inadequate protection against a unilateral take-over or coup by a group that can muster enough naked fire power. We have seen too often military juntas, dictators and revolutionary movements seize office, suspend constitutions, dismiss or imprison elected leaders, declare a state of emergency and give themselves absolute power.

Replacement of Leaders

The second approach calls for the replacement, on a fairly regular basis, of the persons who occupy the positions of leadership. It recognises that the time always comes when those who exercise power have been there too long for their own good and for the good of the organisation. Power has a damaging effect on those who wield it and sooner or later the effects begin to show up.

There is a certain hard-headed realism behind this approach. While it recognises the need to remove corrupted leaders and to replace them by new, and therefore hopefully uncorrupted ones, it knows full well that the new leaders in their turn will eventually be affected by the same contagion and will also have to be replaced.

The replacement of those in leadership can be carried out either peacefully, by means of elections, or violently, by means of revolution or coup. But however it is done, one thing generally remains the same, in neither case are the leaders voluntarily relinquishing power, it is being taken away from them. In a few cases leaders step down or do not seek election but usually the greater majority of those in positions of power will do everything they can to stay in power, and those who do not have power but want it, will do everything they can to capture the positions of power. The only differences are likely to be in the means they use to attain their ends. Too often however, fairness and truth and justice are likely to be early casualties in the struggle.

Chapter 6

The Redemption of Power

One of the themes that Paul deals with in his letter to the
Ephesians is that of the ultimate destiny of the created orders.
God's goal for creation is stated to be

> '... *an administration suitable to the fulness of times, that is,
> the summing up of all things in Christ, things in the heavens
> and things on the earth'* Ephesians 1:10 ASB

The word translated administration is the Greek oikonomia
from which we get our English word 'economy'. Paul is referring to the divine economy. But he also recognises his distinctive role, and that of the church, in this grand design –

> '*to make plain to everyone the administration (oikonomia) of
> this mystery which for ages past was kept hidden in God, who
> created all things. His intent was that now, through the church,
> the manifold wisdom of God should be made known to the rulers
> and authorities in the heavenly realms'*
> Ephesians 3:9–10 NIV

The implementation of the divine economy for creation
necessarily involves the critical issues of leadership and therefore of power, but I suspect that the radical implications of
what is provided in terms of both these factors has never been

understood by the church. Yet the New Testament speaks repeatedly about:

1. A new power and a new power source radically different from all worldly concepts of power and all worldly sources of power.

> *'For the message of the cross is foolishness to those who are perishing, but to us who are being saved, it is the power of God.'*
>
> *'Jews demand miraculous signs and Greeks look for wisdom, but we preach Christ crucified: a stumbling block to Jews and foolishness to Gentiles, but to those whom God has called, both Jews and Greeks, Christ the power of God and the wisdom of God.'*   1 Corinthians 1:18, 22–24 NIV

2. A new kind of leader and a new kind of leadership radically different from anything previously in existence. In one sweep Jesus cancels out all worldly concepts of leadership and styles of leadership, no matter how culturally determined. He says 'Not so with you.'

> *'Jesus called them together and said, "You know that the rulers of the Gentiles lord it over them, and their high officials exercise authority over them. Not so with you. Instead whoever wants to become great amongst you must be your servant, and whoever wants to be first must be your slave —"'*
>
>   Matthew 20:25–26 NIV

When you examine the concepts of leadership and the leadership and power structures in the church today, you cannot but come to the conclusion that we have never taken this word of Jesus seriously. We will come back later to try and grasp its dramatic significance.

Firstly, however, we need to explore more fully what Paul means when he says that Christ is the power of God, and specifically what the Cross has to do with the issue of power because it is not only Christ, it is Christ crucified who is the power of God. Before we can understand what happened in redemption that so affected power we have to be clear as to what power actually is, and we have to see what happened in terms of power in creation and at the fall.

The Nature of Power

Power can be defined as the capacity or ability

> to act or perform effectively
> to have control over the environment, and
> to get done whatever you will to do.

Thus all power rightly and solely belongs to God.

> *'Once God has spoken;*
> *Twice I have heard this:*
> *That power belongs to God:'* Psalm 62:11 ASB

> *'Yours O Lord, is the greatness and the power and the glory and*
> *the majesty and the splendour, for everything in heaven and*
> *earth is yours.*
> *Yours O Lord is the kingdom; you are exalted as head over all.*
> *Wealth and honor come from you; you are the ruler of all things.*
> *In your hands are strength and power to exalt and give strength*
> *to all.'* 1 Chronicles 29:11–12 NIV

Creation and Fall

In Genesis mankind is given authority over the world that God created, that is, the delegated right to exercise power over their environment, to shape it and to alter it so as to unfold its meaning and develop its potential.

> *'God blessed them and said to them, "Be fruitful and increase in*
> *number; fill the earth and subdue it. Rule over the fish of the sea*
> *and the birds of the air and over every living creature that moves*
> *on the ground."'* Genesis 1:28 NIV

But the authority man was given was that of a steward. Thus man is accountable to God for the uses to which power is put and is called to exercise it always in loving obedience to God to whom all power belongs.

In the Fall however, man succumbed to the temptation to reach for autonomy, to be like God and to be the source of his own wisdom and his own power. Satan who said 'I will be like the Most High' said in turn to Eve, 'You will be like God'. The illegitimate grasp for power therefore lies behind the fall of Lucifer and the fall of man.

Among the evil consequences of the Fall, the following are associated with the question of power.

1. The creation mandate turns against God

Man continues to exercise power over creation but now he does it in rebellion. He builds his cities but the city, beginning with Babel, becomes the symbol of man's corporate rebellion against God. Not only does it become the centre of civilisation and wealth and trade and culture, it also becomes the focus of military might, conquest, oppression and idolatry. The city, in other words becomes a 'power'. It is the enduring symbol that the Old Testament uses to describe all man's creations, institutions, organisations, cultures and societal structures. The same structures are described in the New Testament as 'principalities, powers, rulers, authorities, thrones and dominions.'

2. Man loses his spiritual authority over the world

Into the power vacuum thus created, Satan comes. The archon or ruler of the demons becomes the ruler of the world system which he controls by the authorities and powers that he establishes in the heavenly or spiritual realm.

> *'For our struggle is not against flesh and blood but against the rulers, against the authorities, against the powers of this dark world and against the spiritual forces of evil in the heavenly realms.'*
> Ephesians 6:12 NIV

It is significant that the Hebrew word for city also means 'the watching angel' recognising that behind the structural powers represented by the city, stand the demonic powers, the watching angels. Over every city there is a ruling god and the Bible names many of them – for example, Baal, Astarte, Dagon, Moloch, Chemosh, Diana, Rimmon and many others.

The Incarnation

The wonder of God's grace is that he does not abandon his fallen creation, he even maintains the rebellious structures in being else the world would fall into chaos. But he did more. In Jesus Christ God personally entered creation, more than that, he became part of the created order itself in order to redeem it and recover it to fulfil its original destiny. All the great words of salvation have the same theme, the restoration of creation to be the arena of the Father's glory.

In Galatians 4;4, NIV Paul says *'But when the time had fully come, God sent his Son, born of a woman, born under the law, to redeem –* 'What does it mean *'when the time had fully come'*? If we look at the Gospels records from this perspective, we see something very significant. The time into which Jesus came, and the country into which he was born were ones where the 'powers' were at their most blatant and their most ruthless. First century Palestine was in fact, dominated by the 'powers' in every facet of its national and societal life.

These included:

1. A military power. Palestine was a conquered, subjugated country, occupied by foreign troops, the legions of the all powerful Roman Empire.
2. A civil power, in the hands of the ruthless Idumean House of Herod who was responsible amongst other atrocities for the murder of the infants at Bethlehem.
3. A harsh legalistic religious power, the Sanhedrin and the synagogue, that tried to assassinate Jesus because he broke their religious rules and thus challenged their standing.

4. A repressive economic power that farmed out the taxes and bled the country white with unjust and repressive imposts that kept large sections of the population in abject poverty.
5. The power of Satan evidenced by the suffering caused by sickness and demonisation. Turning from the pages of the Old Testament to the New, the sudden outburst of demonic activity is startling to say the least, almost as though the entire nation had come under demonic infestation to a marked degree.

But in the midst of the unchecked tyranny of the powers, Jesus lived an astonishing human life that was absolutely free. The 'powers' could do nothing with him. None of us are free like that, we can all be ultimately controlled by putting sufficient pressure on either of two weaknesses, one is greed and the other is fear. Every person has a price and every person has a breaking point. The carrot and the stick, used with sufficient skill or sufficient force will manage anybody.

But what do you do with a Man who has no greed and no fear? You can't do anything.

Jesus had no greed. When he said, 'Sell what you have and give to the poor' he had done that himself. When he said, *'the foxes have holes and the birds of the air have nests but the Son of Man has nowhere to lay his head'* (Luke 9:58 NIV), I am certain he did not have a woebegone look on his face, I believe he was almost hilarious. He did not want anything for himself.

And he had no fear. He stands up in the boat in the midst of a demonically produced storm that had the disciples so terrified they were almost irrational and he asks *'Why are you so afraid?'* (Mark 4:40 NIV)

What is more he continually demonstrated his freedom and consistently refused to bow down to or yield to the powers. He deliberately and persistently healed on the Sabbath day and he invaded the temple itself to cast out the traders and call the temple back to its rightful role as a house of prayer for all peoples. He brushed aside Herod's death threat with *'Go tell that fox "Behold I cast out demons and perform cures today and tomorrow and the third day I finish my course"'* (Luke 13:32 RSV) and put Rome itself in its place as a penultimate authority *'Render to Caesar the things that are Caesar's and to God the things that are God's'* (Luke 20:25 RSV)

He even went out into the wilderness, faced the strong man, Satan himself, and did the unthinkable, handed him total and unmitigated defeat. *'Away from me Satan, for it is written – "Worship the Lord your God and serve Him only."'* (Matthew 4:10 NIV)

The Cross

But when we come to Passion week, we find the shocking paradox – Jesus surrenders to the 'powers'! He lets the religious power take him prisoner and cross-examine him; the religious power hands him over to the military power that mocks him, flogs him and finally crucifies him, whilst the economic power strips him stark naked on the cross and makes his clothes the prize in a game of dice.

But there was something even stranger. Jesus surrenders to the Satanic power.

He said

> *'This is your hour, and the power of darkness.'*
>
> Luke 22:53 RSV

> *'I will not talk much with you: for the prince of this world cometh, and he hath nothing in me.'*   John 14:30 AV

There was just one moment in the whole of time and one place in the whole of the universe when the devil thought he had everything in his grasp. He had the Son of God, the Eternal Logos, a willing helpless victim in his hands.

But, as ever, Satan reckoned without the ultimate hidden wisdom of God that was in the Cross.

> *'None of the rulers of this age understood it, for if they had they would not have crucified the Lord of Glory.'*
>
> 1 Corinthians 2:8 NIV

61

Paul is speaking of the demonic rulers who engineered the betrayal and death of Jesus. He says that if they had any idea of what was going to take place on the cross they would have levelled every tree in Palestine rather than let one of them be used to crucify Jesus because the results of his death and resurrection were catastrophic for the powers.

1. Firstly the devil is destroyed, that is, disarmed or rendered powerless (katargeo);

I used to wonder what astonished Jesus in Gethsemane. Not the Cross surely? He had always known about the Cross. He set his face like a flint towards Jerusalem knowing that it meant the Cross, but now in the Garden he is appalled by something, distressed and troubled, heavy with loathing and overwhelmed even to the point of death.

Then there was that strange prayer of Jesus, 'Not what I will but what you will', prayed not once or twice but three times before the issue was settled. In all the life of Jesus there had been only one will, the will of the Father. He used to say *'I always do what pleases him'* (John 8:29 NIV) *'My food is to do the will of him who sent me and to finish his work'* (John 4:34 NIV). Yet when he comes to the Garden there is this struggle – my will – your will – my will – your will, in such a moral agony that his sweat became like drops of blood falling on the ground.

I do not know all that went on in Gethsemane. I suspect that there are depths of it we will never be able to plumb in all eternity. But this I begin to understand. When Jesus came to the Garden he took upon himself, not just the guilt of our sins, but our sin.

> *'He made him who had no sin to be sin for us so that in him we might become the righteousness of God'*
>
> 2 Corinthians 5:22 NIV

The root of sin is rebellion against God, the prideful, self-seeking drive for autonomous power, that to this day cannot abide the thought of a God who dares to say 'Thou shalt not –'

Jesus, I believe, became experientially aware in his own

being of how deep and implacable that self-centred power lust ran in the human nature he had come to redeem, and it appalled him. Thus it was not his own will that he struggled with, to make it accept the Father's will, it was our will. In himself and for us he took our rebellious human will, broke it free from its self-centred power lust and made it yield to the Father's will. That is the only thing that makes it possible for us to change in our attitude towards God, from disobedient rebels to loving, obedient sons and daughters.

By dealing thus with the root of rebellion in human nature, Jesus also robs the devil of his hold over the race of the redeemed because he is 'the spirit who is now at work in those who are disobedient.' (Ephesians 2:2) The devil is effectively disarmed as far as their lives are concerned.

2. Secondly, Jesus redeemed power itself. Fallen power that imposes its own will is now brought to yield to the Father's will, power that seeks autonomy, to be its own end and its own God, is faced with a will set in the direction of utter obedience.

> *'He humbled himself and became obedient to death – even death on a cross!'* Philippians 2:8

What Paul stresses was not that Jesus' death on the Cross was something he freely chose himself, but that it was a death chosen for him by the Father to which he was willingly obedient. That choice made by the Man with the most power in the entire universe, did something to power itself – it redeemed it.

> *'Therefore God exalted him to the highest place and gave him the name which is above every name, that at the name of Jesus every knee should bow, in heaven and earth and under the earth, and every tongue confess that Jesus Christ is Lord to the glory of God the Father.'* Philippians 2:9–11 NIV

The Character of Redeemed Power

If redemption has to reach as far as sin has gone, and if power has been corrupted by the fall, then power itself has been one of the objects of redemption. What then is the nature, or what are the essential characteristics of redeemed power, the power exercised by a God who reigns from the cross? What has happened to power to save it from having a corrupting effect on those who wield it? Here are what appear to be its four essential qualities.

1. Firstly, this power has settled forever the issue of obedience to the Father's will.

What happened in Gethsemane and what happened on the Cross has formed it forever in the direction of 'Not as I will but as you will'. In other words it is power that is permanently bent in the direction of obedience to God, in contradistinction to worldly power that is perpetually twisted towards self-seeking.

2. Secondly, with this power the distinction between means and ends has been settled once and for all.

The one and single end and the only goal of every activity in which this power participates is the Father's glory. Everything else is merely a means to that end. Thus it strives for success, but success is not its goal; it seeks to achieve, but achievement is not its objective; it works for results, but results are not its aim. Its purpose is only to glorify the Father and if doing that leads through weakness and persecution and affliction and apparent failure, it is content with its lot.

3. Thirdly, this power has embraced the Cross and in Christ has died out there to all self seeking, self glorification and the will-to-power.

That is the weakness that Paul embraced, and embracing it discovered the way in which this power is perfected.

> 'But he has said to me, "My grace is sufficient for you, for my power is made perfect in weakness." I will all the more gladly boast of my weaknesses, that the power of Christ may rest upon me.'　　　　　　　　　　　2 Corinthians 12:9 RSV

> 'For he was crucified in weakness, but lives by the power of God. For we are weak in him, but in dealing with you we shall live with him by the power of God.'　　　　2 Corinthians 13:4 RSV

4. Fourthly, this power has a radically different orientation, it is wholly power for others, not power for self nor power over others.

It is his experience with this kind of power that lies behind some of the astonishing assertions of the apostle Paul, like 1 Corinthians 4:8–13, that otherwise we find difficult to take at face value and read either as sarcasm or irony. They are neither.

> *'For we who are alive are always being given over to death for Jesus' sake, so that his life may be revealed in our mortal body. So death is at work in us, but life is at work in you.*
>
> 2 Corinthians 4:11–12 NIV

Chapter 7

The Redemption of Leadership

In the process of redemption Jesus not only brings into existence a new and redeemed type of power, he creates and models
a new kind of leader to handle that power. Both are necessary
because you cannot join the new creation to the old any more
than you can safely put the new wine into old wineskins. In
other words the old type of leader cannot understand, let alone
handle the new kind of power, nor can the new kind of power
do the sort of things the old type of leader usually wants
to do.

When Jesus said *'Not so with you'* (Matthew 20:26 NIV) he
cancelled out the legitimacy of all existing concepts of leadership. In their place he introduces the only type of leader who
can safely be entrusted with power without being corrupted by
it. That leader is one who:

1. Is a servant by nature, and

2. Has got beyond the status syndrome.

The implications of this model of leadership are staggering.
Can you imagine what sort of society we could produce if every
major institution and organisation were led by men and women
who could be trusted to use power rightly and not to be spoiled
or corrupted by it?

Servant Leaders

In Matthew 20 Jesus deals with this crucial aspect of the question of leadership. The setting is one of the all too familiar struggles that come from the will-to-power. Two of the disciples, James and John have just decided to make their bid for the most powerful positions in the Kingdom, the one on the right hand and the one on the left hand of the King. To present their case they have called in the best and most enthusiastic advocate they could find – their mother. Ambition, particularly when attracted by power, will use any means and any methods to attain its ends.

Not unexpectedly there has been a burst of indignation from ten other power-seekers who suddenly see their own private ambitions in danger of being upstaged.

Then Jesus calls the disciples together and says,

> *'You know that the rulers of the Gentiles lord it over them, and their high officials exercise authority over them. Not so with you. Instead, whoever wants to be great among you must be your servant, and whoever wants to be first among you must be your slave – just as the Son of Man did not come to be served, but to serve and to give his life a ransom for many.'*
>
> Matthew 20:25–28 NIV

Most leaders, if they are honest, will confess, as I do, to being both puzzled and also irritated by this passage, because Jesus seems to be trying to link together, not only two different roles but two mutually exclusive roles. After all, leaders lead, servants serve. If leaders are going to be the servants what are the servants going to do, and who is going to do the leading? We probably have much more sympathy with the viewpoint expressed in the following passage because it seems more in accord with common wisdom.

> *'Will any one of you, who has a servant ploughing or keeping sheep, say to him when he has come in from the field "Come at once and sit down at table?" Will he not rather say to him,*

"Prepare supper for me, and gird yourself and serve me, till I eat and drink and afterward you shall eat and drink"?'

Luke 17:7–8 RSV

How then are we to understand the radical juxtaposition of ideas that Jesus introduces – the leader who is also, or even primarily a servant? It is inescapable that Jesus meant it to be taken seriously because he not only taught it, he modelled it and he pointed to himself as the example we should follow.

Robert Greenleaf in his seminal book Servant Leadership makes some perceptive comments that provide a good introduction to the subject and a first rate commentary on these words of Jesus. There are, he says, two kinds of leaders. Firstly there are the strong natural leaders. In any situation they are the ones who naturally try to take charge of things, make the decisions and give the orders. Generally they are driven by assertiveness or acquisitiveness or dominance. But secondly there are the strong natural servants who assume leadership simply because they see it as a way in which they can serve. If things are ever going to change for the better in our society, says Greenleaf, only natural servants ought to lead and we should refuse to be led by anybody who is not a natural servant. Furthermore, the biggest obstacle to change in society is natural servants who have the capacity to lead, but don't.

Nature, Not Activities

The first thing that we have to get clear is that we are dealing with a question of character or nature, not a question of function. The servant leader is first and foremost a servant by nature, it is what he is, not merely what he does. Servanthood is the motivation that drives his behaviour, and motivation is all-important in a servant. A person can carry out all the duties or functions of a servant, or do the tasks that a servant has to do, but do it unwillingly or resentfully or just for the money. The person on the receiving end of what is being done soon becomes aware of the lack of real service.

Often a person genuinely and willingly serves but sees

service as a means to an end, that end being to rise to a position where you no longer have to serve people but have other people serving you. Therefore they serve wholeheartedly all the time they are on the way up, but when they get to the top they turn into tyrants. They somehow reckon they have paid their dues by waiting on other people, now it is their turn to sit back and give the orders and watch other people jump to it for a change.

Leaders can also get involved in a lot of serving activities without ever being servant leaders. Some undertake all manner of tasks and duties but it is a burden to them. They refuse to delegate because they never seem to be able to find people they can trust to do the job properly, yet they grumble all the time about how hard they work and how much they have to do. They end up so busy doing everything themselves that they have no time or energy to lead and are conscious that in spite of all their hard work they are failing.

Other leaders take on a multiplicity of activities and responsibilities, not because they want to serve but in order to make themselves indispensable, because when they are indispensable they wield real power. The threat, or even the hint of them withdrawing their services is usually enough to deal with any opposition because everybody knows that without them the whole organisation would grind to a halt. It is even possible to get mileage both ways, to enjoy the power that comes from being irreplaceable and at the same time indulge in self pity at being grossly overworked on behalf of people who do not appreciate all the things you do for them.

Nature, Not Leadership Style
We must also emphasise that servant refers to the leader's nature not to leadership style. There are leaders who are task oriented and leaders who are people centred, there are leaders who are highly directive, leaders who function collaboratively and leaders who are democratic in their decision-making styles.

There is compelling evidence that the way we relate operationally with other people is part of our pattern of motivational gifting and therefore is largely innate. We will always try to relate in that manner and will lead most effectively in that way. On the other hand what is the most effective style for a particular occasion is also situationally determined. For example when things are going very well people are content with highly centralised, directive leadership. When things are going very badly the same style of directive, hands-on leadership is the best for taking hold of a hopeless situation and turning it around. In between those two extremes however the more consultative, participative style of leadership seems to produce the best results.

Servant leadership can be found right across the entire continuum of leadership styles, or it can be absent, regardless of the style adopted. Servanthood is the quality of nature or character or motivation.

Nature, Not Role

Finally because servanthood refers to the leader's character or nature, it is not affected or changed by the role they fulfil. They can be given leadership and it can be taken away from them; they remain servants. They can take up leadership and lay it down; their nature never alters. Their inbuilt natural motivation is simply to serve. If they find they can serve best by leading, they will lead. If they find somebody else who can lead better, or they can serve better in another role, they will pass over leadership without a single pang and happily become a follower again. Either way they can fulfil their natural motivation which is to serve.

The Essence of Servanthood

One of the primary biblical images of leadership is the leader as shepherd, because the shepherd is there for the sake of the flock, it is not the flock that is there for the sake of the shepherd. It is the shepherd who lays down his life for the sheep (John 10:11) and the judgment of God against the false shepherds of Israel is that they have been feeding themselves when they should be feeding the flock. (Ezekiel 34:2)

In more specific terms leadership that springs from a true servant nature will manifest the following characteristics.

1. The servant leaders' paramount aim is always the best interests of those they lead.

That means that the leaders have to really know and understand their people so that they know what the people's best interests are. It means that when the people's best interests are known they have priority over the leaders' best interests. That is what it means by laying down your life for the sheep.

2. The servant leaders' paramount satisfaction lies in the growth and development of those they lead.

Often the personal growth and maturity of people is hindered because leaders hold back or keep to themselves the insights and principles and keys to successful ministry as though these were the trade secrets that guarantee their leadership position. Contrast this with Paul's unabashed delight in the progress and success of his churches.

> *'We ought always to thank God for you brothers, and rightly so, because your faith is growing more and more, and the love every one of you has for each other is increasing. Therefore among God's churches we boast about your perseverence and faith…'*
> 2 Thessalonians 1:3–4 NIV

3. There is a willing acceptance of obligation.

Leaders do not generally like to be obliged to do things, they like to be free to decide; they put other people under obligation. That is what makes it very hard to lead leaders. They are strong on commitment but generally they are thinking about other people being committed to them, or to their goals or objectives.

Servants have no problem with obligation, or duty. They are accustomed to doing things, not because they want to do them but because they are required to do them as part of their service. The willingness to accept obligation is one of the hallmarks of servanthood. Paul had it. *'I am bound both to Greeks and non-Greeks, both to the wise and the foolish.'* (Romans 1:14 NIV)

4. The servant leader has a desire for accountability.
There is a difference between accepting the principle of accountability and seeking it. Servants like to be accountable, they are accustomed to being answerable for their performance because they want to know whether they have satisfactorily met the requirements of those they serve.

It is not the natural inclination of leaders to want to be accountable. Their tendency is more in the direction of independence and freedom of action, thus the attitude of leaders towards accountability and answerability is often a good indication as to whether they have the heart of true servanthood.

5. The servant leader has caring love for those he leads.
Care is love, not of the emotions but of the will; it is expressed in action and it has regard for people's needs, their sensibilities, their convenience and their best interests. It is here that the biblical image of the leader as shepherd merges into the image of the leader as father because father is supremely the source of caring love, that knows needs before they are asked (Matthew 6:8) that gives the child what is good for him (Matthew 7:11) and rewards intention rather than results. (Matthew 6:4)

6. The servant leader is willing to listen.
Servants listen because they have to find out what it is they have to do. Leaders don't listen – they speak and others listen. But the Servant of the Lord, who is also the Messianic King says:

> *'He wakens me morning by morning,*
> *wakens my ear to listen like one being taught,*
> *The Sovereign Lord has opened my ears*
> *and I have not been rebellious.'* Isaiah 50:4–5 NIV

The servant leader is always listening because he too wants to know what he ought to do. He is listening to God but he has learned that God not only speaks directly, he speaks indirectly through people. Therefore the servant leader is open to receive criticism and advice. Anything you can tell a servant that will help him to do a better job is welcome because at the end of the day the results are what counts and the servant would rather be commended than scolded.

Leaders often become defensive or belligerent at any suggestion that their performance could be improved by doing this or that. The attitude of the servant leader however, is 'If you can show me anything that will help me to make a better decision, now or the next time, then I want to know.'

7. Servant leaders have genuine humility of heart and because of that a realistic and sound judgment as to their capabilities and their deficiencies, the things they can do well and the things they cannot.

8. Finally the servant leader is willing to share power with others so that they are empowered, that is, they become freer, more autonomous, more capable and therefore more powerful. He has learned, perhaps intuitively at first and then by experience that the more people there are who have power, the more power there is, and that if this is to happen then nobody or no group of people should have all the power and nobody should be without any power.

Chapter 8

How to Become a Servant Leader

We have tried to clarify the answer to the first important question to be asked about servant leadership, that is, 'What does it mean?'

We come now to the second and equally important question, 'How do you do it?' or more accurately, since we are talking about a nature or a character, 'How do you get it?' Unless we can answer this question satisfactorily we will either be frustrated by seeing an ideal that seems unattainable, or we will fall into the error of thinking that if we only understand the concept we can do it, or be it.

The Source of the Servant Nature

To get something you have to go to the right source, and as far as the nature of the servant leader is concerned, there is only one source and that is Jesus Christ. Jesus makes that very clear himself.

> *'Just as the Son of Man did not come to be served, but to serve and to give his life as a ransom for many.'*
>
> Matthew 20:28 NIV

> *'For who is greater, the one who is at the table or the one who serves? Is it not the one who is at table? But I am among you as one who serves.'*
> Luke 22:27 NIV

Probably the most astonishing picture of all in the Gospels is in John 21. There we find the risen Christ, the conqueror over sin and death and Satan, and the One to whom all authority in heaven and on earth has been given – on the beach and cooking fish for the disciples' breakfast.

But Jesus also brought that servant nature down so that it would be accessible to us. Paul explains the process step by step in Philippians 2 and emphasises that it is meant to be experiential in us.

> *'Your attitude should be the same as that of Christ Jesus'*
> Philippians 2:5 NIV

Attitudes are the things that determine what we are like and how we act and react. Attitudes are more than beliefs because beliefs are purely intellectual views we hold to and beliefs rarely affect our way of life. Attitudes are made up of

1. A cognitive element, that is intellectual beliefs or convictions.
2. An emotional element, feelings we have about these beliefs,
3. A volitional element, that is behavioural responses we make because of our beliefs.

His Way to Servanthood

The passage in Philippians needs to be analysed very carefully. Here is what it says

> *'Who being in very nature God,*
> *did not consider equality with God something to be grasped,*
> *but made himself nothing,*
> *taking the very nature of a servant,*
> *being made in human likeness.'* Philippians 2:6–7 NIV

In whatever terms we are to understand the kenosis, the

divine self emptying of the Son of God, the following facts are inescapable.

1. Jesus was 'in very nature God', which means he was fully and completely God, deity was his nature and his being.

2. He made himself nothing, literally 'emptied himself' – it was something Christ did deliberately, willingly, knowingly and actively. He emptied himself of certain things and he took to himself other things.

3. He took the nature of a servant, which means he was as fully and completely a servant by nature as he was God by nature. He was not merely acting like a servant or doing servant things, servanthood was his nature. That is why all his acts of service came naturally to him, there was nothing forced or strained or artificial about them, they flowed spontaneously and authentically out of what he was in himself.

4. That servant nature was a human nature, injected into the bloodstream of humanity, as it were, so that it could become accessible and available to us in Christ.

5. Then, Jesus took that servant nature, and exposed it to all the stresses and circumstances of human life, building into it all the capacities we would ever need and proving it in all the challenges we would ever have to face. And then –

> *'Being found in appearance as a man,*
> *he humbled himself*
> *and became obedient to death –*
> *even death on a cross!*   Philippians 2:8 NIV

One of the conditions of human existence appears to be that death seals it in its essential moral state. After death no radical alteration is possible, the only changes that take place are that we become more and more of what we then are. *'Let him who does wrong continue to do wrong; let him who is vile continue to be vile; let him who does right continue to do right; and let him who is holy continue to be holy.'* Revelation 22:11 NIV

The death of Jesus sealed his human life in its immortality as Paul points out in Romans 6

'For we know that since Christ was raised from the dead, he cannot die again; death no longer has mastery over him. The death he died, he died to sin once for all; "but the life he lives he lives to God"'　　　　　　　　　　　　Romans 6:9–10 NIV

But since the dominion of death is sin, sin has no mastery over the risen human life of Jesus. **Death sealed his human nature in its sinlessness. By the same token it sealed it in its chosen servant nature** so that he is still, exalted King of Glory though he is, the Son of Man who is amongst us as one who serves.

Experiencing the Servant Nature of Christ

Our access to the life of Christ comes through the new birth, the work of regeneration. Our experience of living by the power of that life comes through the work of sanctification. What this latter work means for us is the following:

1. Coming to an increasing understanding and appreciation of what has been accomplished for us in:

(a)　The work of the Cross
(b)　The work of the Holy Spirit in applying the work of the Cross.

2. An increasing and continuous appropriation of the reality of that work for ourselves; 'reckoning on it' to use Paul's term.

3. Learning, in moral and spiritual issues, to make continual deliberate choices that are in harmony with that reality.

Understanding

The first stage is understanding. Hopefully we are at least on the way to grasping the truth that in the Incarnation Jesus created a servant nature, and became a servant, and that through our incorporation in him in his death and resurrection we can come in touch with and into union with that nature. But we need to reflect deeply and ponder the truth until it becomes revelation to our hearts.

Appropriation

The second stage is appropriation. Here, deep issues will be worked out within our hearts therefore it is not something to be rushed through. Indeed it cannot be rushed through or nothing will happen. What we face is nothing less than walking through the same stages and the same steps as Jesus walked through, because

> *'A student is not above his teacher nor a servant above his master. It is enough for the student to be like his teacher and the servant like his master.'*　　　　　Matthew 10:24–25 NIV

In one sense it is a very personal journey and a very subjective experience, therefore no two people will do it in exactly the same way or face exactly the same issues. Philippians 2 does however give some general map references to help chart the way and show us how far on the journey we have got.

1. *'Not something to be grasped'* (verse 6).

Once we open our heart to the searching scan of the Holy Spirit we will undoubtedly come to the realisation of certain deeply cherished goals and worthy ambitions that have become for us personally 'something to be grasped.' We cannot let other people stipulate these categories for us and we are forbidden to try and determine them for other people, but we will arrive at inescapable, sometimes heart-wrenching clarity about the specific issues that the Holy Spirit is putting his finger on.

The first stage is giving up those things that we have been grasping, and reckoning them as no longer to be sought for, or striven for, or considered as a legitimate end or goal of our endeavours.

2. *'Made himself nothing'*: that is, emptied himself.

We will then come, if we do not draw back, to a place of self emptying where we also let go of our ambitions and our agendas, our visions and our dreams and of the position we hold, or desire to hold in the opinions of others. In other words we let go of the whole apparatus of the will-to-power. It means we rid ourselves of all our investment or stake in things like success, status, position, rank or reputation.

But there is more to it than that – we have to empty *ourselves*. That means abandoning our strengths and our abilities, even though they are God-given, our self confidence and our proven track record, our learning, our experience, our self conceits and our positive self image, in fact the whole paraphernalia that feeds our fallen vanity and makes us imagine we are something or somebody. We may think we are rejecting the things that constitute our self but what is going is not our real self but all the things within us that power can seduce or position can flatter.

To be sure, the self-emptying of the Son of God had nothing in common with ours. His was the laying aside of perfections, of immaculate goods, ours is the emptying of strengths, all of which are tarnished and ambiguous, and potentials, all of which are flawed and fallen.

3. 'taking the very nature of a servant'
When are we ready to appropriate the servant nature of Christ? Only when the process of self-emptying is completed, because right up to this point servanthood is only a concept to us, and we are not dealing with concepts, we are dealing with life. Only the Holy Spirit knows when we have completed that stage and he alone can bring us to the realisation that at last the old has gone and now the new can come.

At that point also, the how-to of appropriation becomes crystal clear. We understand what it means to 'take', to 'put on' or to 'receive', it becomes simple to 'reckon on' and to 'walk by the Spirit', they are suddenly terms we can understand and act upon. I suspect that one of the chief reasons why we find a lack of reality in 'putting on' is because we have not yet dealt properly with 'putting off' and therefore have not reached the point of faith where appropriation is possible.

4. 'he humbled himself and became obedient to death'.
Receiving the servant nature is usually a crisis experience,

walking in it is a process, the heart of which is the divine commandment

> '*Do not use your freedom to indulge the sinful nature; rather, serve one another in love.*
> *The entire law is summed up in a single command: "Love your neighbour as yourself."*'
> Galatians 5:13–14 NIV

Continuation

It is very important to understand the way God works in our life to effect character change. Firstly, he is concerned with inner change, not the kind of things I do but the kind of person I become. For example he does not want me to go around doing kind deeds all the time, he wants me to become a kind person. When I am a kind person everything I do will be stamped with kindliness, even when it is reproof or discipline. God does not want me to go round speaking the literal truth out on each and every occasion, he wants me to become a true person, then there will be an integrity about everything I do or say. Therefore he is also not concerned about me going around doing servant things all the time but having a servant heart.

Secondly, in the Bible, God has not given us detailed, specific instructions on how to handle every situation or set of circumstances. There is no set of rules and regulations, or any ready-made system that will automatically tell us what to do on every occasion. The weakness of having a set of rules is that, like the Pharisees, we can always find a way to live comfortably with the letter of the law without allowing it to affect our heart or challenge our motives.

Instead God has:

1. Set out his commandments in the form of principles to guide our behaviour
2. Given a few specific examples or applications to give some teeth to the principles, and
3. Left us to apply the principles as creatively and as honestly as we can to the real life situations we face.

This is not living with a set of laws but living in harmony with our servant nature and asking in every situation, 'What course of action in these circumstances will advance the best interests of those I lead?' There is no fail-safe method of getting it right every time. Many times our choices will be ambiguous and our judgment astray, and we will have mistakes aplenty to learn from. But of this we can be sure – living by the principles God has laid down will in the long run achieve his purpose for us. Being a servant, and if we are leading, a servant leader, becomes second nature to us. In other words we do it naturally and spontaneously so that whether we are making the decisions, or carrying out someone else's decisions, issuing instructions or obeying orders, pioneering something new or facilitating someone else's vision, we do it to serve.

Chapter 9

The Status Syndrome

We come now to consider the second characteristic of the kind of leader Jesus introduced who can be trusted to handle power without being seduced or corrupted by it. It has to do with the sensitive issue of status.

Status is about our ranking or position in society in comparison or in relation to others. Jesus told a trenchant parable about status when he was invited to dinner and saw the invited guests scrambling to grab the places of honour at the table.

> *'When someone invites you to a wedding feast, do not take the place of honour, for a person more distinguished than you may have been invited. If so, the host who invited both of you will come and say to you, "Give this man your seat". Then humiliated you will have to take the least important place.*
>
> *But when you are invited, take the lowest place, so that when your host comes, he will say to you, "Friend, move up to a better place". Then you will be honoured in the presence of all your fellow guests. For everyone who exalts himself will be humbled, and he who humbles himself will be exalted.'*

Luke 14:8–11 NIV

Status and Leadership

In the world, leadership and status go hand in hand. In a business corporation you can almost always tell who the

82

President or the Chief Executive is, because he has a bigger office than anyone else, and it is generally on the top floor of the building. He also has a bigger desk than anyone else and a thicker carpet than anyone else, and a parking place nobody else can use. How essential are any or all of these for the job he has to do? They are not actually necessary at all, they are status symbols.

Status is one of the main non-monetary rewards of leadership, sometimes it is the main reward. People will accept the demands and difficulties inherent in a leadership position, they will put up with the onerous responsibilities and the heavy time commitment, they will sacrifice other worthwhile interests and sometimes even accept lower financial rewards, just to bask in the status that goes with the job.

Sometimes status is offered as a substitute for monetary rewards. Call a clerk an office manager or a mechanic an engineer and you may actually get them to turn down a better paid job elsewhere because they would revert to the lower status terminology again.

Status is not only sought after, it is assiduously protected by the position holders. You will have noticed how sensitive some of them become if protocol is not observed or recognition is not given, even if they rationalise their reaction as not being a personal matter but having to do with respect for the office they hold.

Status is also used to reinforce the power of leadership by deliberately creating vertical distance between leaders and followers. Thus the orders and decisions of the leaders come 'down' from the top, as though they thereby carry an extra weight of authority and descend from the demi-gods, and demi-goddesses who inhabit the rarified atmosphere of the upper echelons of the organisation. When you allow yourself to think about it, it all seems ridiculous pretence of course, but it is given credence by the careful use of status symbols and status-loaded language.

There are times however when status is not so much sought by the leaders as given to them by the people they lead, even forced on them whether they want it or not. People today are the same as the people in Samuel's day who wanted a king, and one like all the other nations.

> *'that our king may govern us, and go out before us, and fight our battles.'*
> 1 Samuel 8:20 RSV

The reasons for this are not far to seek. Give the king or leader power and status and then he and he alone is responsible for results. If he succeeds, people can identify with him and therefore be a part of a success with the minimum of effort and inconvenience. On the other hand, if he fails, he can carry all the blame, because if he gets the bouquets he can also take the brickbats.

Even David found this out to his cost when the Amalekites took the city of Ziklag in his absence and carried off all the wives and families of his men.

> *'David was greatly distressed because all the people spoke of stoning him, because all the people were bitter in soul, each for his sons and daughters.'*
> 1 Samuel 30:6 RSV

Status effects not only the leader but the leader's wife. There are certain expectations made of the church leader's wife, and certain attitudes adopted towards her, just because she is the pastor's wife, or the elder's wife. I know many women in such positions to whom these things are a great burden. It also extends to the leader's family, and many times it is the hidden agenda against which the preacher's kid is rebelling.

The Effects of Status

Status has the effect of accentuating and reinforcing many of the damaging influences of power on those who wield it.

Firstly, the deference it creates, feeds pride and fosters vanity and conceit. The leader is in great danger of beginning to believe the flattering things being said about him or her.

Secondly, the distance it establishes between leaders and people encourages arrogance by subtly inducing in the leaders the sense that they somehow belong to an elite, superior to other people. From that it is a short step to believing that they ought not to be challenged or questioned or that the standards and moral restraints that apply to other people do not apply to them.

Thirdly, the personal aggrandisement that status adds to all the other rewards of power makes the involuntary loss of office often so costly that it virtually ensures that the office holder will try to hold on to the position by fair means or foul.

Manifestations of Status

The manifestations of status and the range of status symbols in use are legion. The following are a few representative examples so that we can begin to see how pervasive the concept of status is and how much it has penetrated our thinking and even our language. Many of the marks of status can be found in the Church, functioning as fully and effectively as in the world, used in the Church for the same purposes, and sadly with the same effects.

1. Special means of identification such as titles, special forms of address or distinctive clothes. It is not the identification of roles or offices as such that I am referring to, or even the means used for that purpose. In many circumstances they are a simple matter of organisational necessity. But when, for example, we use some of these titles as a form of address and not others, the reason turns out on examination to be a matter of status. I do not call the church organist, 'Organist Smith,' then why do I call the minister 'Pastor Smith,' or the Bishop, 'Bishop Smith' or 'My Lord Bishop'?

2. Often leaders receive special privileges, that other people in the organisation do not receive, for example first class travel, accommodation at top class hotels, chauffeur driven cars, entertainment allowances and so on.

3. Sometimes status is expressed in higher monetary rewards. This may be difficult to establish because of the problem of measuring the relative worth and value of different jobs but even in a free market economy it is obvious that the rewards that are attached to certain positions are affected to a considerable extent by the status of the position and on occasion the status of the person holding the position. Issues of relativity between professions or trades that cannot be directly compared in terms of their activities, revolve very much around the question of status. If one group in one industry gets an award increase it has a domino effect on all other groups which feel they must maintain their parity or they have lost status.

4. Deference given to the leaders' opinions outside the area of their competence. The opinions of leaders on anything and everything from politics to Bach and baseball are treated with seriousness and great respect just because they are the leaders. They may be talking the most arrant nonsense, but it is a brave soul that has the temerity to point that out. What keeps us silent? The awe of status.

5. Access to the leader is strictly limited. Ordinary people can get an audience or get access only on certain matters or only through prescribed channels and after running the gauntlet of secretaries and personal assistants. A new incumbent who inherits the job finds that he also inherits with it a team of people whose main function in life is to protect him and his time from the intrusion by lesser mortals.

Such conditions are by no means absent from the church. Prominent speakers can have their personal assistants who run interference for them to save them from being buttonholed by all and sundry, and presumably being asked questions beneath their notice by people beneath their notice. The disciples tried it just once with their Rabbi, to protect his privacy from mothers with their babies and little children, and got smartly put in their place: *'When Jesus saw this'*, we read, *'he was indignant'* (Mark 10:14 NIV)

6. Leaders are given a kind of representative signifi-cance. If the organisation or the team achieves noteworthy results or attains its objectives, it is the leaders who are singled out for acclaim or praise, as though they were solely or pri-marily the ones who were responsible for the achievement. 'A special vote of thanks to Mr Joe Bloggins and "his" team for their wonderful achievement in doubling the sales figures.' Joe Bloggins modestly admits that 'he' could not have done it all without the help of his fifty perspiring salesmen. Language is very revealing of our attitudes; for example, when did you ever hear a special vote of thanks being given to 'Sales Department B and its manager Joe Bloggins'? Actually, you find it, or something very like it in Paul's letter to the Philippians. He addresses it, *'to all the saints in Christ Jesus who are at Philippi, together with the overseers and deacons'* (Philippians 1:1 NIV) If the Philippian church leaders had any illusions about status, they must have been instantly dispelled when they opened that letter!

What Jesus Did With Status

There is an incident in John chapter 13 that some years ago had a revolutionary impact on our whole understanding of leader-ship in the church eldership to which I belonged. It is no exaggeration to say that it liberated us as leaders in a way nothing had ever done before.

Jesus has just finished washing the disciples' feet and then he asks them a question.

> *'When he had washed their feet, and taken his garments and resumed his place, he said to them, "Do you know what I have done to you?*
> *You call me Teacher and Lord; and you are right, for so I am. If I, then, your Lord and Teacher have washed your feet, you also ought to wash one another's feet. For I have given you an example that you should do as I have done to you".'*
> John 13:12–15 RSV

Why, we might ask, did the disciples not wash one another's feet? It was not because it was a dirty job, but because it was a menial job; it was a low status job, the job of a slave.

What does Jesus say? 'You call me teacher and Lord, and you are right, for so I am'. I like that! He knew that he was the Leader, and he made no bones about it. But he had washed their feet. In so doing he had demonstrated this radical principle –

Leadership is a special function but it carries no status with it whatsoever.

I wish that I could communicate the liberating impact of that realisation. You see, in the church there are many leaders who have reacted against the whole status thing. There are also very many people who have reacted against the status given to leaders and the authoritarianism that it both produces and reinforces. Sometimes the reaction has been against leadership in any shape or form. 'We are not going to be led by man, we are going to be led only by the Holy Spirit.' Sadly, people who have been badly scarred by authoritarian dominance are not often in the best position to listen to the leadings of the Spirit or to discern them aright. The result is a situation that is going nowhere because no lead is being given.

But now we understand that leaders have to lead, that is their job. But as a job it is no more important than any others and it carries no special status at all. Leaders can climb down off the pedestals on which they have been placed and can lead with all their heart and with all their energy. That is what they are there for, but their perspective and their functioning need no longer be cluttered up with status symbols.

True, there are differences in the various roles in an organisation. There are some things that leaders do that others don't do, and there are some things that others do that leaders don't do. But status is not one of them. Now for the first time I begin to understand some of the previously rather cryptic sayings of Paul – *'greater honour to the parts that lacked it'* (1 Corinthians 12:24 NIV) or *'us apostles as last of all'* (1 Corinthians 4:9 RSV)

Nor is the question of status to be confused with the honour or respect that is to be given to leaders for a job well done. *'Let the elders who rule well be considered worthy of double honour'* (1 Timothy 5:17 RSV)

Honour is the recognition of value and therefore honour is always mutual from people to their leaders and from leaders to their people.

> Servanthood for followers is honouring their leaders and obeying them. (Hebrews 13:17)

> Servanthood for leaders is honouring their followers and laying down their lives for them. (John 10:11)

Dismantling the Status Syndrome

Freedom from the status trap must begin with leaders and it must begin with a change in heart attitude. When that change takes place it is like chains dropping off. The whole thing loses both its seductive power and its crippling constraints. I remember one prominent evangelist telling me how after he had spoken at a meeting and given the altar call he used to leave by the back of the stage so as not to get involved with little old ladies who wanted to be seen talking to the visiting speaker. He actually had an assistant to intercept such advances. He realised that he had been caught in the status trap – maintaining the certain aloof distance from ordinary mortals that belonged to his role as the 'man of God'!

Then it becomes an educative process. We have to start dismantling the symbols that affect us personally and teaching our people to step free of them too. You will be surprised how much it does to bridge the distance between leaders and people. Leaders in churches often think there is no distance between them and their people, and from their perception that may be true. But talk to the people and you will generally find that there is an enormous distance. The leaders or the elders are 'the heavies', they are those spiritual giants away out there who do their own thing and pay little attention to lesser mortals. Please do not think that this is an exaggeration and does not apply to your church.

How are we to recognise status symbols? Conditions and circumstances differ so drastically from one situation to another that rules of thumb are notoriously unreliable. Personally, I ask myself one question, 'Is this intrinsic or extrinsic to my job?' In other words do I really need this to do my job properly or is it a disposable extra?

One leader may need some protection from interruptions or he may need to have notice in advance of a caller's purpose in order to do his job properly. Then those things are intrinsic needs, they are not status symbols. A leader may need an extra large room and comfortable seating because she customarily deals with large planning groups in lengthy meetings. That is not a matter of status.

But if there are special perks or privileges that are extrinsic, that is, they have nothing essentially to do with the effective carrying out of my job, then for me I would have a fear that they could become a pleasant, attractive, seductive status symbol that would feed my vanity, pander to my conceit and expose me to the dangers of the lust for power. That I would rather be without.

Chapter 10

Coping With Criticism

One of the things leaders often find hard to handle is the criticism and questioning to which they are often exposed. They get frustrated and baffled by it, sometimes hurt and bitter. But criticism is rarely very far away, leaders find it attached to the job like a permanent price tag – only nobody ever warned them about that beforehand. Therefore there is value in examining the subject with some care.

Criticism can come from opponents or adversaries, it can come from leaders in other churches or Christian organisations, or it can come from within our own ranks, from the very people we are trying to serve and lead.

Criticism from outside is easiest to handle. After all, we reason, our assailants must have a personal axe to grind and we can put their attacks down to prejudice, ignorance, spiritual blindness or wilful opposition to the truth. There is even something bracing about it, a sense of being in the firing line of the spiritual war.

Coming from fellow Christian leaders, criticism is harder to bear because we are supposed to be on the same side in spite of differences in denominational labels, doctrines or worship styles. But we can always explain it in part to ourselves as narrowmindedness or insecurity or even jealousy.

Criticism from within our own ranks is the worst of all because here we really are on the same side and complaint or criticism smacks very much of disloyalty or rebellion. We can be excessively hurt when it comes from some of the very people who only a couple of years ago called us into leadership and begged us to take on the job. Suddenly our most avid supporters have become our detractors. We feel betrayed, decide we can never really trust anybody and wonder if we should take them on at their own game and fight fire with fire.

Why Does Criticism Arise?

It will help us to deal more objectively with criticism if we realise from the start that it is an inevitable part of the environment that surrounds the role and function of leaders. As the saying goes – If you cannot stand the heat you had better get out of the kitchen. A necessary characteristic required of leaders is the strength of purpose to press on and accomplish whatever they have set out to do, even in the face of negative feedback. If they lack this capacity, they will end up not leading at all but merely following the public mood of the moment.

We must go further however, and realise that not only is criticism something that leaders always have to face, it is also understandable and perfectly legitimate even when there has been no failure on the part of leaders. We need to see why this is so.

1. Leaders, if they are doing their job properly, are generally dealing with change, and to most people change is uncomfortable and often threatening, even when it is a change for the better. Therefore the status quo will always have its resolute defenders who resist change for no other reason than that it is change and who see the leaders as being the instigators of their discomfort.

2. Leaders are dealing with the future and working towards goals and objectives that lie in the future, therefore the present is always incomplete and the objectives only partially accomplished. Thus there are always legitimate criticisms that can be made, and genuine deficiencies and inadequacies that can be pointed out. Even when the current goals are reached, and

even if they are perfectly accomplished, the leaders if they are doing their job, are already on their way towards the next set of goals, so that again there will be shortcomings and incompleteness that can be criticised.

3. Criticisms and questions often arise simply because people cannot see the future as clearly and as compellingly as the leaders can. Nor are they to be expected to, otherwise they would not need leaders, or they themselves would be the leaders. The leaders' task is to articulate the vision and keep on pointing the way ahead and the existence of questions and doubts may only mean that they are not doing this job adequately.

4. There may be criticism because people do not have access to the full information possessed by the leaders and are drawing conclusions from inadequate data. This often arises because leaders are not communicating clearly enough or fully enough or sometimes because they are deliberately withholding information as a means of establishing and maintaining their power.

5. In difficult times the vision wanes. When the going gets tough, obstacles and obstructions begin to loom larger and more convincing than the goals. The problems are real and present while the goals are still away off in the future. Fear-based questioning and grumbling are common. The story of the Exodus ought to be required reading for all leaders, not least of all for what it can teach us about the dynamics of criticism. The journey to any goal of significance has its trek through the wilderness. But that is exactly where leaders are needed. When things are going well, anybody can lead, leaders can even feel superfluous. It is when things are going badly and everybody else is ready to call it a day and go back to Egypt – that is when leaders come into their own.

6. Sometimes criticism is voiced because people see genuine dangers and mistakes that leaders have overlooked. The truth of the matter is that absorption with and commitment to long term goals can sometimes render leaders blind to tank traps right under their feet. Immediate and short range dangers are sometimes detected more clearly by those not in leadership.

93

7. Questioning occurs because our perception of situations is different and that in turn is because our basic motivation is different. Thus the person who requires a clear and precise definition of a task before he can get going will always be asking for more specifics, the person who is a problem-solver will always be looking for potential problems and the person who needs time to prepare for something new will always resist an immediate response.

8. Leaders handle power and used carelessly, power can maim. It would be easy to fall into despair at the trail of hurt and scarred Christians damaged by authoritarian, insensitive or often just careless leaders. Many of these people find it impossible to trust any leadership again because they have been so injured. It takes discernment to perceive, and wisdom to deal with the criticism that comes from woundedness.

9. Again because leadership handles power, and therefore appears glamorous and exciting, it can even invoke jealousy amongst those who would like to be leaders and are not, or who have aspired to the position and have been passed over or rejected. Jealousy or envy can come out in criticism or personal attack as it did against Moses. *'In the camp they grew envious of Moses, and of Aaron who was consecrated to the Lord.'* (Psalm 106:16 NIV)

10. Finally we often criticise just because it is very much easier to find fault than to create. To initiate or build something is difficult and requires time, energy and the willingness to take risks. Moreover there is often a lot at stake, even if only the initiator's reputation. But, as Gene Edwards says 'The ability to see faults is a cheap and common gift.'

Criticism is also an attractive option, for another reason. It carries the unspoken implication that we would have done much better that what has been done, without us ever having to demonstrate whether we could or not.

How To Handle Criticism

Once leaders have realised that there is nothing unnatural or necessarily damaging about criticism, and that in any case they are going to have to learn to live with it, the question is, what is the best and most creative way to handle it. Here are some basic ground rules.

1. Don't reject it out of hand

We have already mentioned that leaders must have the courage and strength of purpose to keep on course even in the face of negative feedback. This comes easier to the leader who by nature or temperament prefers to ignore opposition and press on regardless. Such an automatic approach to criticism or questioning is, however, never to be recommended for the very good reason that it can easily lead to arrogance or foster an overbearing attitude. Arrogance, and the deception to which it leads are so deadly that leaders should be thankful for any criticism no matter how unreasonable because at the very least it is a protection against these major dangers.

2. Don't be discouraged by it

Criticism can easily sap leaders' courage, especially when it comes from within their ranks or from people they have come to depend on for support or whose good opinion they value. Sometimes there will be other people or peers to whom leaders can turn for reassurance but in the ultimate they have to dig down to find a source of strength and courage within themselves to face the situation. That means finding our strength in Christ and the assurance of His presence. In the disaster at Ziklag when David's own men were talking of stoning him we read *'But David found strength in the Lord his God.'* (1 Sam 30:6 NIV)

3. Don't be demoralised by it

Demoralisation is a step further down the track of discouragement. It happens when leaders, hemmed in by opposition and difficulty are tempted to take an unethical or unprincipled course of action because it offers a seeming opportunity to get off the hook. Or it can happen when the external pressure of criticism and opposition become too great and the leaders' fortitude or courage or will to resist suddenly snaps. Then we need what Paul prayed for:

> *'I pray that out of His glorious riches He may strengthen you with power through His Spirit in your inner being.'*
>
> Ephesians 3:16 NIV

4. Don't be ruled by it

Sometimes leaders are tempted to yield to criticism and to alter plans or policies for the sake of peace and quiet. In the church this is often rationalised as being for the sake of unity. Usually all that happens, however, is that the alterations arouse new opponents from amongst those who were content with the previous policy and are now upset with the changes. The leaders try a middle course to placate both sides only to find that neither are happy with the compromise. What is more, the previously silent majority now becomes disenchanted because they see the leaders 'playing to the gallery' and bending to whichever pressure group is most vocal.

This is not by any means to say that the approach to criticism should be one of inflexible unyieldedness, but it is to point out that short term adjustments merely to placate criticism can lead us astray from legitimate long term goals.

5. Don't personalise it

This is probably the most important 'don't' of all, and the hardest to abide by. Leaders can err here in two ways. Firstly they can take criticism of their policies or their plans as being personal criticism and therefore an attack on their integrity or character or capability. Secondly they can react personally against the critic and reject the person as well as the person's views or opinions.

Always address criticism on its objective merits and as relating to an objective matter. The attitude of leaders must always be 'If you can help us to make a better decision we are open to your help and grateful for it.'

Even a wrong motive behind a criticism is not sufficient

grounds for it being automatically rejected. Honesty compels me to admit that there are times when exactly the wrong person at exactly the wrong time with exactly the wrong motives has nevertheless said exactly the right thing.

6. Seek to discover the reason behind the criticism

Many times a criticism or the way it is expressed does not represent the real problem but is only a result or a symptom of the real issue. Discovering the real reasons that lie back of a question or a criticism will often condition the response that is appropriate in the circumstances. The same thing said by different people may need quite different responses. For example, the reason for a particular criticism may be:

(a) Fear of change or fear of the future. In this case what is called for is reassurance.

(b) Mistake, misunderstanding or lack of comprehension. This calls for information or explanation or enlightenment.

(c) Loss of heart in the face of difficulties or defying circumstances. The need is for the people affected to be encouraged and reassured.

(d) Perceived error or danger. The criticism needs to be heeded and action taken to correct the fault or avoid the threat.

(e) A diversion, or a profitless dispute that will achieve nothing. The criticism needs to be refuted otherwise it will dissipate people's energies and obstruct progress.

(f) An expression of hurt or woundedness because of what the person has experienced from leaders, present or past. In some cases leaders may need to acknowledge responsibility, seek forgiveness and bind up the wounds. In other cases, there may be a need for healing although no blame attaches to the leaders, for example, a person who has been passed over for a position they desired may be hurt thereby even though the decision was a correct one.

(g) Wrong attitude or a wrong spirit, for example, envy, jealousy, contention or divisiveness. These need to be opposed. At the same time leaders must be wary of characterising criticism as being wrongly motivated when the reaction to it may be their own defensiveness, or pride or insecurity.

The best advice is that conclusions as to motives and attitudes should be cautiously and tentatively arrived at out of honest endeavours to treat the situation under one or other of the other heads listed above. But deciding motives should never be the first assumption; we are rarely able to be sure of even our own motives and therefore generally poorly placed to judge others.

Facing Personal Attacks

What happens when criticism becomes a personal attack? Sometimes criticism of leaders can degenerate to personalities or even a form of character assassination when it becomes clear that not the policies but the leaders as persons are the target of an attack. The important issues in such cases are as follows:

1. Don't give as good as you get. When the spirit behind the criticism is wrong it can only be overcome by responding in a contrary spirit –

> If it is driven by contention – respond in peaceableness
> If it is driven by malice – respond in love
> If it is driven by meanness – respond in generosity
> If it is driven by pride – respond in humility
> If it is driven by arrogance – respond in teachableness
> If it is driven by deception – respond in truth
> If it is driven by mistrust – respond in faith

2. Don't allow your emotions to dictate your responses so that you are speaking out of hurt or anger. Similarly don't become resentful or bitter or fall into the sin of self pity, the 'poor me' syndrome. Remember that there are probably others more vulnerable than you are to the effects of the attack, for example your spouse and family.

3. Don't become the personal focus of a division. Division is rarely, if ever, a fruitful resolution of a problem but if division ever becomes necessary it should be accomplished peaceably and should be because of principles that in good conscience cannot be satisfactorily resolved within one group or one objective. It should never be division over personalities.

4. Don't allow others to be attacked through you and don't distance yourself from those to whom you owe loyalty when they are under attack. Loyalty means 'I am for you even if others are against you and I will defend you even at cost or risk to myself.'

Chapter 11

Authority – The Leader's Mantle

Leaders are inextricably involved with authority. One of the things that people instantly recognised in Jesus was that he had authority. He spoke with authority, he acted with authority, he taught with authority, and when he commanded, even demons, wind and water obeyed him. And by his death and resurrection he has obtained all authority, in heaven and on earth, spiritual and temporal. (Matthew 28:18)

But one of the things we struggle with is that although authority is an essential attribute of leadership, and leaders cannot function effectively without it, yet at the same time the misuse of authority is one of leadership's main failings and the source of the most persistent complaints made against leaders.

The Terminology of Power

Any discussion of the subject of authority also brings in two other related concepts, power, and responsibility. They are often not clearly distinguished because the terms are not used in a consistent way; for example some writers use power and authority as interchangeable and others use authority and responsibility as referring to the same thing. But the concepts need to be kept distinct to be clear, therefore we will use the terms with the following meanings:

Power

Power (Gk dunamis) is used to describe intrinsic strength or ability. It is the dynamism or potency that enables a person to get people to do something or to change in some way whether they want to or not, or to get things done in the face of opposing or defying circumstances.

The kinds of power that leaders may exercise have been variously analysed. One useful, if not exhaustive, classification is as follows:

1. Reward Power.

This is the power that leaders have to reward behaviour that they desire or want to see take place. Leaders may, for example, have the power to promote, to give salary increases, to make awards or appoint to special offices, or to grant other assistance. They can then exercise considerable indirect influence over the way people behave, by either granting or withholding benefits that are at their command. Even the leaders' power to publicly commend or acknowledge achievement is a form of reward power.

2. Coercive Power.

This is the opposite of reward power; it is the ability to threaten or punish those who do not behave in the desired manner. They may be demoted, fined, dismissed, expelled, imprisoned or have other unpleasant sanctions used against them. The power of leaders to reprimand or rebuke is also, in a milder form, an example of coercive power.

3. Expert Power.

This is the power that comes from having superior skill, strength, knowledge or ability. The expert has power because he or she can do a task better than anyone else or knows more about a subject than anyone else.

Leaders may be personally expert in certain areas of skill or knowledge without having expert power, because the particular expertise is irrelevant to the job in hand. In fact it is not really necessary for them to have expert power in any area except one, and that is leadership. It does not matter if other people can do any or all of the jobs in the organisation better than the leader, but no one should be able to lead as well as the leader can.

4. Legitimate Power.
People recognise power as being legitimate when its norms, that is what it stands for, agree with their own set of inner values. Thus if the people's concept of leadership in the church is that it should be collaborative and people centred, they will tend to regard as illegitimate and authoritarian, any form of leadership that is centralised, task oriented and directive. On the other hand if people view the church as a hierarchical institution where the role of leaders is to say what ought to be done, they will recognise the right of the leader to make unilateral decisions as perfectly legitimate and reject the more people centred styles of leadership as being weak and ineffective.

Authority

By authority we mean two things, firstly the right to exercise power, and secondly the actual exercise of that power. In other words there is no authority if power is not delegated to back it up and there is no authority if it is not used. Jesus gave the seventy disciples power and authority to drive out all demons and to heal sicknesses, and the disciples went out and used that authority. The result? They returned with joy and said 'Lord even the demons submit to us in your name.'

Responsibility

By responsibility we mean accountability for performance or answerability for results. Some people want the right to use power but they do not want to be responsible for the outcomes. Other people avoid leadership positions because they do not want the responsibility.

Power, authority and responsibility not only go together, they must be equal. That means that:

1. Those who are charged with exercising authority must be given enough power to do it. There is no point in giving a person formal authority if there is insufficient power to back it up.

2. Those who are given power and authority must be held fully responsible and accountable for the results, otherwise you will get power used irresponsibly.

3. Those who are held responsible for results must be given sufficient power and authority to do the job properly.

All three elements are to be found in the parable of the talents in Luke 19:

Power is represented by the talents or minas given by the noblemen to his servants.

Authority was given by his instructions – 'put this money to work until I come back.'

Responsibility was required when the nobleman returned and called the servants to account for what they had done with the talents.

Authority and Obedience

God's purpose has always been for man to exercise authority as can be seen from the original mandate or stewardship he gave to humankind to rule over the world. (Genesis 1:28) But because authority is delegated power, it can be used only by those who are in obedient relationship to the source of that power. The Roman centurion who so impressed Jesus, and was so impressed by Jesus understood that perfectly. He did not say, 'I myself am a man with authority', he said, 'I myself am a man under authority, with soldiers under me.'

> *'I tell this one "Go", and he goes; and that one "Come", and he comes. I say to my servant "Do this", and he does it.'*
>
> Luke 7:8 NIV

The centurion knew that he had authority over his 100 men as long as he himself stayed under authority. His men obeyed his orders unquestioningly, because they knew that if they disobeyed the centurion, his superior would back him up, and his superior's superior would do the same, all the way back to Caesar on his throne in Rome. All the power of Rome stood behind the centurion, as long as he stayed under authority. If he stepped out of that obedience, he lost all his authority.

True authority is spiritual in origin, that is, it proceeds from the spirit of the one exercising it and it impacts on the person over whom it is exercised, also in his spirit. It carries an 'oughtness' about it that registers on the person's conscience, but, and this is important, it leaves his will free to choose to obey or disobey.

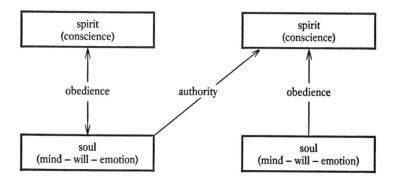

When those who are exercising authority are not themselves living in obedience to a higher authority – what happens? In that case what comes out is not authority at all, but willpower, emotional pressure or forceful argument. Because all these have their origin in the soul, it will impact on the other person's soul also. There will be a clash of wills, conflicting arguments or opposing emotions. The person being given the orders will either give way under the force of stronger soul power, but feel resentful or bitter, or he will stand up for himself and there will be open conflict.

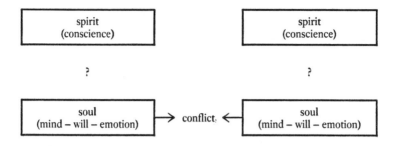

When I choose to obey true authority I do not feel inferior or put down in any way because true authority is spiritual and respects my moral freedom. Obedience is my free choice. But when so-called authority seeks to impose another person's will on mine or brings emotional or intellectual pressure to bear it does not respect my moral freedom. I can conform or rebel, and neither is likely to bring any real satisfaction.

Situational Analysis of Authority

In considering the whole question of authority, the aspect that is nearly always overlooked is the nature of the situation in which authority is being exercised. Yet these situational aspects have a very important influence on the kind of authority that should be used, and indeed of the kind of obedience that is the appropriate response. A type of authority that is perfectly suitable in one kind of situation may be inadequate in another situation and inappropriate, even dangerous, in another. This section is particularly important for church leaders because by the nature of things they deal with the same people but in often very different situations or circumstances and you cannot therefore use merely one uniform kind of authority.

Three typical categories of situations can be identified, namely Task situations, Teaching situations and Ethical or spiritual situations, and the type of authority appropriate to each is classed as Task Authority, Teaching Authority and

Spiritual Authority. When we turn to the New Testament we find that the different words used for obedience and disobedience can be fitted very closely into this analysis, as below.

Type of situation	Task	Teaching	Spiritual
Aim	To do	To learn how to do	To learn to be – character change
Hearers required	To understand instructions	To understand reasons for the instructions	Conviction of the conscience
Nature of obedience	peithearcheo = to submit to one in authority	peitho = to be persuaded	hupakouo = to listen under
Disobedience	anopotaktos = unruliness	apeitheia = to be unpersuadable	parakoe = refusal to listen

The Nature of Task Authority

This is the simplest and most direct form of authority and it treats the subordinates as merely extra hands or other capacities at the service of the person in charge. The leader gives directions and instructions and all that is required of subordinates is that they understand the orders and carry them out as accurately as possible. With one mind running things and co-ordinating the efforts of all, the team can do far more than the leader could do alone.

In task situations therefore, leaders do not expect to have to give reasons justifying their decisions, nor are they very interested in discussion or reaching consensus as to what is to be done. Their authority tends to be simple, directive and categorical.

Task authority is a legitimate and appropriate type of authority that works perfectly well in the following types of situations.

1. It is the first type of authority used with small children and is used to establish their obedience where there is not yet a

basis for understanding the reasons why the orders are given. If you do not want your little toddler to go out on to the road, you have to rely on task authority because he is too young to understand the danger, nor can he be expected to. He has to learn to obey, just because you told him.

2. Task authority is also appropriate for the large number of fairly simple and straightforward jobs that have to be done, or those that call for co-ordinating the efforts of a group of people. If there is a heavy crate to be lifted, somebody has to decide when to say 'Heave', it does not call for a committee meeting.

Similarly when large numbers of people are involved in an operation or have to be moved within a short period of time, task authority does the job best.

3. Task authority also remains the best, perhaps even the only type of authority that can handle emergencies, or dangerous, high risk situations where communication is difficult, for example battlefield conditions. These situations however call for a very high degree of implicit trust in the leaders, therefore known and tried leaders are preferred, or the people involved have to be drilled in the instant and unquestioning obedience that is often necessary for survival in such circumstances.

Task Obedience

The New Testament word for obedience is peithearcheo which means to submit to one in authority. (Acts 5:29, Titus 3:1); disobedience is anopotaktos, unruliness (1 Tim 1:9) which must always be checked or it will lead to ineffectiveness, disorder and worse.

Limitations of Task Authority

If task authority is used too long with children, or if it is used inappropriately, it can hold people down in psychological immaturity, sometimes to the extent that they become unable to make decisions on their own or take responsibility for their own lives. One of the criticisms levelled against much of the task authority in industry is that it does just that. Adult men and women on the factory floor spend their working lives under a type of authority that belongs to their early childhood.

Furthermore task authority is usually strictly limited to the task in hand. It does not give the leaders authority over the actions of their subordinates outside the scope of the task. It often requires considerable adjustment for this to be recognised and for the quality of relationships on the job not to spill over into private and social life.

The Nature of Teaching Authority

Teaching authority differs fundamentally from task authority because its aims are different. The aim of task authority is to get something done, whereas the aim of teaching authority is that somebody learns how to do.

The word authority comes from the Latin augere – to make increase or make grow. Thus in the realm of knowledge an authority is a person who makes others grow by what he knows or what he contributes. The authority of the teachers lies in the fact that they stand in a relationship of familiarity with or mastery of the subject they are trying to communicate. They have first hand access to it. Learners submit to the teachers' authority because they do not have first hand access to the body of knowledge, but only through the teachers.

The teaching authority thus has two tasks. The first is to bring the knowledge down until it is within reach of the learners. This involves simplification, explanation and illustration. The second is to raise the capacities of the learners so that they can reach the body of knowledge in greater depth or sophistication.

Teaching authority cannot therefore rely merely on clear or explicit instructions or directions. It must go on to uncover the reasons and the principles behind the instructions. It follows therefore that questions, discussion, objections, arguments and explanations are not only permissible, they are part of the learning process. Teaching authority has not done its job properly until the reasons are not only clearly communicated to the learners but fully understood by them.

This points out the inadequacy of task authority in a teaching situation. At most it will produce rote learning or learning 'parrot fashion'. Learners will often be content with this but real teachers will never allow this to happen but will insist that the learners struggle with the reasons and the justifications because only when these are grasped can they be said to have begun to master the subject.

Morever teaching authority is knowingly self limiting; its aim is always to become redundant, which happens when the learners acquire their own direct access to the body of knowledge and no longer need the teachers. The ambition of every true teacher is that their pupils will in time surpass them, otherwise the knowledge of the teacher becomes a ceiling past which the learners cannot go.

Obedience to Teaching Authority

The basic authority of leaders in the church is teaching authority therefore they are bound to give reasons and explanations for what they preach and teach, and be prepared to be freely questioned by those they lead. The New Testament word for obedience in this context is peitho which means 'to be persuaded', and to persuade means to win over or to bring about a change of mind by the influence of reason or moral considerations. It is the word used in Hebrews 13:17 NIV:

> *'Obey your leaders and submit to their authority. They keep watch over you as men who must give an account. Obey them so that their work will be a joy not a burden'*

Disobedience is apeitheia, the condition of being unpersuadable, or the obstinate refusal or rejection of truth. (Titus 3:3)

The Nature of Spiritual Authority

Authority exercised in the spiritual or moral realms is different from either task or teaching authority because again, its aims are different. If the aim of task authority is to do, and the aim of teaching authority is to learn how to do, then the aim of spiritual authority is to learn to be, in other words it is concerned with character and character change.

Because it is concerned with character, spiritual authority must be deeply committed to:

1. The integrity of moral choice, and therefore the necessity for people to decide and make choices on the basis of conscience. In fact, in moral or spiritual issues, if a person is not deciding on the basis of conscience they are not acting morally at all, they are acting non-morally. No matter how socially desirable their decision may be it is conformity not morality that is guiding their behaviour.

2. The honouring of individuality and difference so that people are not expected to fit into a standard pattern where they all think the same way, respond the same way and talk the same way. God's way is not uniformity but unity-in-diversity.

3. Respect for personal privacy. God honours the integrity of personal choice and personal privacy even when it shuts him out of people's lives. (Revelation 3:20) We must honour it in the same way.

Obedience to Spiritual Authority.

The New Testament word for obedience here is hupakuou, which means to listen under. (Romans 6:17, 2 Corinthians 10:5) It has the same sense as the Hebrew shema which means to listen intelligently. In both cases it is listening not merely with the ears but with the conscience.

Disobedience is parakoe, the deliberate refusal to listen:

> *'For this people's heart has become calloused;*
> *they hardly hear with their ears,*
> *and they have closed their eyes.*

Otherwise they might see with their eyes,
hear with their ears,
understand with their hearts and turn
and I would heal them'   Matthew 13:15 NIV

The Purpose of Spiritual Authority

Some of the wisest words ever written on spiritual authority come from Menno Simons, one of the founding fathers of the Mennonite Church. They were written in Reformation times, which makes them even more remarkable, because that was a time when theological opponents were generally burned at the stake. He said,

> 'Spiritual authority is never to make the rebel conform; its only purpose is to enable the obedient person to live a holy life. Therefore it rests on submission and obedience freely given. Furthermore, spiritual authority has only spiritual means at its disposal; its only weapons are prayer, scripture, counsel and the power of a holy life.'

Church leaders who are exercising spiritual authority must therefore strenuously avoid coercion and manipulation in any form whatsoever, whether by force of will or personality, charisma or reputation, or group or peer pressure. Even more to be shunned are claims to divine revelation or divine sanction to back up directives or reinforce views or opinions.

But they must also avoid allowing people to delegate their moral responsibility upwards. There is a dangerous tendency in some people to avoid personal moral responsibility by trying to get their leaders to make the ethical decisions for them. They will come and say 'You are a man of God, you tell me what to do and I will do it'. 'You are a woman who knows God and I trust your discernment, please tell me what is the right thing to do'. It can be very flattering and very tempting but it must be avoided like the plague. You cannot be another person's conscience and you cannot be God to him or her.

When faithfully exercised and willingly received, spiritual authority fulfills the following three purposes in the church:

1. To exercise Christ's authority in the heavenly or spiritual realm. God's will is done by God willing it in heaven, and man willing it on earth.

    > *'I have given you authority to trample on snakes and scorpions and to overcome all the power of the enemy, nothing will harm you'*
    > Luke 10:19 NIV

2. To give authoritative and reliable, but not infallible, guidance and direction to the church (Acts 15:1–19), and,

3. To make disciples, not to men but to Christ

    > *'All authority in heaven and on earth has been given to me. Therefore go and make disciples of all nations.'*
    > Matthew 28:18 NIV

Misuse of Authority in Moral and Spiritual Situations

We have already said that task authority in a teaching situation is inadequate. To that we must now add that task authority in a moral or spiritual situation is deadly. It produces legalism, the letter that kills.

> *'He has made us competent as ministers of a new covenant – not of the letter but of the Spirit; for the letter kills but the Spirit gives life.'*
> 2 Corinthians 3:6 NIV

When spiritual leaders declare categorically what they conceive to be the truth in moral or spiritual matters, and allow for no questioning, no inquiry and no discussion, they are using task authority in a spiritual situation. And when they classify any contrary views or alternative interpretations as rebellion against anointed authority they are also misusing task authority.

Task authority in spiritual matters and the ethical issues that go with them, inevitably produces legalism.

There is a difference between law and legalism. The deadly peril of legalism is that it enables us to find a way to live within the letter of the law without it affecting our heart. The Pharisees had established some 300 rules on sabbath keeping, if you kept them all, not even God could accuse you of a breach of the sabbath. But the spirit of the sabbath commandment, man's vocation to live for the glory of God, could be avoided altogether.

Legalism, by shielding us from the impact of the law, also produces moral insensitivity. If I handle the law the way it is meant to be handled I will soon discover that it is a two-edged sword that will smite me first and more than it smites my hearers. Legalism on the other hand, allows me to smite someone with the letter of the law and not be touched by it myself at all.

Chapter 12

Biblical Stress Management

Stress is the term that is used to describe the strain and tension that people experience when they are in situations that are inharmonious or dysfunctional or that effectively prevent or hinder them from doing the things they want to do, or achieving goals that are important to them.

There are certain characteristics of the leaders' role and function that of themselves tend to create stress quite apart from any thing else that is going on. Leading is thus always among the high stress occupations, for the following reasons:

1. Studies have clearly shown that all change produces certain levels of stress, even when it is a change for the better. Leaders are always dealing with change.

2. As we have already seen, criticism is an inevitable component of the leaders' environment, and disapproval or fault finding or complaining is often very hard to handle.

> *'For I have heard the slander of many,*
> *Terror is on every side;*
> *While they took counsel against me,*
> *They schemed to take away my life.'*   Psalm 38:19

3. Leaders are carrying the weight of responsibility. They are aware of being answerable for the way their decisions work out and accountable for the results of their policies. That is

why many people avoid leadership roles because they do not want to carry that load.

4. Christian leaders are in a very strategic and often very exposed place in the spiritual battle that rages. In Mark 3:27 Jesus states a very important principle – first tie up the strong man, then you can rob his goods. What we often overlook is that Satan understands this principle also, therefore his attack is particularly focused on disabling the leaders in any work of God.

The Burden of Negative Reactions

Often leaders experience guilt or a sense of failure when they find themselves letting things get on top of them or when they realise they are reacting less than adequately to pressure and stress. They can panic or become confused as to why it is happening or even resentful that they have this extra problem to face on top of everything else they are carrying. And they can feel very isolated, as though nobody else has ever been through this and therefore nobody understands what it is like.

It is reassuring to such people to discover that the apostle Paul understood all the effects of being in a high stress occupation. What is more, he made no secret about both his outer and his inner experiences as a Christian leader. He says things like, 'I was depressed'; 'I was really scared', 'I was under such pressure I thought I was going to die'. What is more, the church he shared these things with was not his favourite church at Philippi, or the church at Ephesus into which he had poured so much of himself, but the carnal, squabbling, undisciplined bunch of charismatics at Corinth that took so much of the apostle's time in trying to keep them on the right track!

We have reason to be grateful for Paul's honesty however, because in revealing his struggles he also clarifies a number of very important biblical principles for managing stress. It is these inner principles that we need to get hold of and apply. Relaxation methods, time management skills, prioritising of tasks and other behavioural technologies that are often taught as ways of enabling people to handle stress are not without their value. But the reality is that they probably do little more than raise our stress threshold. Manifestly something more is needed.

Sources of Stress

A study of 2 Corinthians gives us Paul's perceptive taxonomy of the types of stress to which Christian leaders are exposed and also the principles that carried him successfully, if sometimes painfully, through these experiences. These principles can also help us in similar situations.

Stress Caused by Difficult Circumstances or Difficult People

In 2 Corinthians 1:8–11 NIV Paul speaks about 'affliction', that is the stress and suffering that comes our way through difficult and defying circumstances or the opposition and antagonism of people.

> *'We do not want you to be uninformed brothers, about the hardships we suffered in the province of Asia. We were under great pressure, far beyond our ability to endure, so that we despaired even of life. Indeed in our hearts we felt the sentence of death. But this happened that we might not rely on ourselves, but on God who raises the dead. He has delivered us from such a deadly peril, and he will deliver us. On him we have set our hope that he will continue to deliver us, as you help us by your prayers.'*

We do not know the particular circumstances to which Paul is referring here. Perhaps it was the riot described in Acts 19, or the time he 'fought with wild beasts at Ephesus.' (1 Corinthians 15:32) But he is undoubtedly speaking about the pressure and stress that occurs when adverse circumstances seem to pile up against us without let up and there is the added suffering caused by the malevolence of people who are against us. But through it all Paul establishes three powerful principles for handling the stress caused by adversity.

First principle: It is at the extremities of our strength that we run into God's strength.

I remember some years ago at a Bible School class we were studying the gift of prophecy and part way through the class I said, 'That is enough theory, now we are going to do some practice.'

So the class closed their note books and we began to worship the Lord. A spirit of prophecy came on that class and I heard people prophesy that night that had never opened their mouths in that way before. What is more God began to say some really profound things. One of them I have never forgotten. Round about that time God had been saying to us as a church, 'I want to do something new among you.' That night God said, 'I cannot do the new thing while you are still living within your capacity.'

It was almost as though there was a perimeter, that represented the furthest out I had ever reached in faith, the furthest out I had ever reached in commitment and the furthest out I had ever gone in obedience to God. But that is a scary place to live. You are never sure what is going to happen out there. So we pull back just a little. Now I am living within my capacity. Now things are more under control.

God's new things do not happen within our control, nor is it there we meet the power of God. The power of God always operates at the margins. It is when we run out of our capacity that we run into His.

Moreover God, I discover, will do nothing to get me from where I am now out to the perimeter. He already knows I can get there. I already know I can get there, I have been there. Therefore access to divine power and strength necessitates:

Firstly, that in whatever circumstances I am, I brace myself willingly to take the strain. I always have the choice as to how I am going to face the pressure, either braced like a combatant, or limp and helpless, as a victim.

Secondly, at the margins, at the limits of our capacities, we look to run into God's capacities. This means digging down inside yourself until you tap into the apparently inexhaustible well of resurrection life that is in the indwelling Spirit. As you get towards the limits of your reserves, it gets harder and harder, and more and more likely to be impossible. Push out a step beyond the margins and you suddenly run into resources that you know do not have their source in you but in God.

Principle 2: Past deliverance gives secure grounds for future hope (v10).

In other words, in the bad times, remember the good times. Paul is emphasising the importance of recall – remembering our past experiences of God's faithfulness and God's intervening mercy. The prophets of Israel were always doing this. In the darkest days they rehearsed again and again, God's saving acts. 'Remember how he delivered us from Egypt. Remember how he opened the Red Sea. Remember how he fed us on manna and brought water out of the rock. Remember. Remember.'

> *'Yet this I call to mind*
> *and therefore I have hope:*
> *Because of the Lord's great love we are not consumed,*
> *for his compassions never fail.*
> *They are new every morning; great is your faithfulness.'*
> Lamentations 3:21–23 NIV

The importance of remembering lies in our tendency to absolutise the present. If things are going well, I may blithely assume they will always be like that and fall into presumption or carelessness. If things are going badly I can easily feel they will always be like that and fall into despair. Therefore in the good times we probably need to remember the bad times and certainly in the bad times we need the encouragement of rehearsing the good times.

I remember a businessman friend telling me of a particularly difficult time he was going through when he had almost lost hope and none of his prayers seemed to be making any difference. One Sunday afternoon he sat down with a scratch pad and began to jot down a record of the times when he had seen God's supernatural intervention in his business affairs. He was amazed to find he could recall over 150 such occurrences.

Principle 3: In your need turn towards the body for its prayers.
Leaders tend to have certain particular strengths and capacities and they are needed for their job. One is the ability to keep going when everybody is ready to give up. Another is the confidence to stand and carry the day alone if need be. But these strengths can also become weaknesses. Particularly common amongst Christian leaders is an independence that keeps its problems to itself and presents an image of self sufficiency to the church. Very often God uses trouble to deal with our independent spirit. Some of the most significant times in my life have been when I have had to stand in front of my people and say, 'Please pray for me or I don't think I can make it.'

Paul, I discover, prayed for his people. More than that, he told them he was praying for them. More than that, he told them what he was praying for them. More than that, he asked them to pray for him. Most Christian leaders, I discover, have no idea of the enormous reservoir of genuine regard and concern there is towards them from their people, too often dammed up, because the image the leaders present is that they do not need it, and can manage without it.

Years ago an Anglican woman in a church in Auckland, New Zealand, said something to me that has affected my whole view of ministry ever since. I had taken a weekend seminar in her church, and she said, 'You have really helped us a lot this weekend, Tom, because we can identify with your weaknesses.' I have never forgotten that. People do not identify with our strengths or our successes. They may admire them, they may envy them, but they do not identify with them. But our weaknesses are our point of contact with people because they can recognise them in themselves and find we share the same struggles.

Stress Caused by Our Human Frailty

In 2 Corinthians 4:7ff NIV Paul talks about the pressure and stress we experience just because of the limits and frailty of our human nature.

> *'But we have this treasure in jars of clay to show that this all-surpassing power is from God and not from us. We are hard pressed on every side but not crushed; perplexed but not in despair; persecuted but not abandoned; struck down but not destroyed. We always carry around in our body the death of Jesus, so that the life of Jesus may also be revealed in our body.'*

It is not certain whether the earthen vessels Paul refers to are the little pottery lamps that people used, very cheap and very fragile, or the earthen jars in which they often kept their valuables. Nevertheless the point is clear – Christians are never explicable in purely human terms alone, there is a treasure within.

But the treasure is contained in very ordinary, very frail and very fragile containers. You are not superman or superwoman or superpastor. The human body and the human psyche have limits and if they are stretched beyond those limits we will suffer. If the stress is unduly prolonged we may incur harm or damage. In this passage, however, Paul lays down the three principles for personal survival when we are caught in situations like this.

Principle 1. Remember that God always sets the limits to what happens to us. (v7–9)

Some years ago I wrote an article for our magazine in which I referred to this passage and said, 'The Christian is never the victim of chance, or circumstances, or demons or any combination of them. In everything God is working and over everything God is sovereign.'

About six weeks after the article was published my first wife was driving in our car one Tuesday morning and was hit by a heavy truck. She died in hospital that evening without regaining consciousness. A week or two later, in the middle of the struggle to find answers to the questions that were raging in my heart, I remembered what I had written. I felt trapped, I had said it, I had gone into print and now I was being asked, 'True or False?' I remember the anguish I went through at the very bedrock of my existence. Was my wife's death an accident, a mere evil chance or was it the devil? One man who wrote to me thought that our spiritual armour had not been in place properly that day and the devil had got under our defences. Or was it divine providence God's sovereign decision to answer in one moment all my wife's longings for His presence?

One morning as I was praying I found myself saying, 'Father, if I really knew it was your will to take Jenny home I think I could accept it.' It was one of those times when God speaks very clearly. He said, 'You will never understand my will from outside it, you will only understand my will from inside it.' I said, 'Lord, how do I get inside your will?' He said, 'You will never get inside my will by just accepting it – you only get inside my will by embracing it.'

That morning I was able to reach out and embrace the Father's will, and only then did I begin to feel solid ground under my feet. It took me safely through between rebellion on one side and dull fatalism on the other. I may even have found the key to the age old controversy over divine sovereignty and human freedom, that they are existentially harmonised when man reaches out and freely embraces God's sovereign will. This I now certainly know, that when we embrace God's sovereign will for our life, all the circumstances come under His providence, and that providence sets the limits as to what happens to us. On this my heart has found a resting place. God's sovereign providence sets the limits, on that we can rely.

Principle 2. Remember the Cross principle of sacrifice.

> *'For we who are alive are always being given over to death for Jesus sake, so that his life may be revealed in our mortal body. So then death is at work in us, but life is at work in you.'*
>
> 2 Corinthians 4:11–12 NIV

This is the biblical principle of death and resurrection, life out of death, that Jesus spoke about in John 12:24 NIV

> *'I tell you the truth, unless a grain of wheat falls into the ground and dies, it remains only a single seed. But if it dies, it produces many seeds.'*

But there is a very important qualifying principle that we must never lose sight of, that is, only the God-ordained death leads to resurrection. It was not Jesus' death as death that resulted in resurrection, it was his death willingly embraced as the Father's will that led to resurrection.

If we decide of our own volition to put something to death, a work, a ministry, a relationship or a church – all we will end up with is death. Over the years I have seen all these things done, more than once. Certainly, if God put his hand on anything, whatever it is, and ordains its death, let it go to death, because resurrection will always be the outcome. But never do it yourself.

Principle 3. Remember the steadying influence of the divine perspective.

> *'Therefore we do not lose heart. Though outwardly we are wasting away, yet inwardly we are being renewed day by day. For our light and momentary troubles are achieving for us an eternal glory that far outweighs them all. So we fix our eyes, not on what is seen but on what is unseen. For what is seen is temporary, but what is unseen is eternal.'*
>
> 2 Corinthians 4:16–18 NIV

Paul was able to survive and to overcome gloriously in harrowingly difficult circumstances because he had an eternal perspective against which he could measure all that happened to him. The usual effect of increased stress is that we lose our perspective. Troubles fill our whole horizon, obstacles grow in our mind to insurmountable proportions. Paul says, 'Get the eternal perspective and you see things quite differently, what you find is that trouble is working on our side, it is actually producing for us.'

Our emotional responses are largely governed by our perceptions. Perceive something as a threat and you will experience fear, even if, in fact, there was no danger at all. Perceive something as humorous and you will want to laugh, even if the experience is painful. I remember a Catholic student one night telling me about the run up to his final law exams. He had worried himself sick, sitting up night after night at his books and keeping himself awake with pots of coffee. But straight after his last papers he went climbing in the New Zealand Southern Alps and a couple of days later found himself high up amongst the snowy peaks. Suddenly amongst that grandeur his anxieties over things like examinations shrank to miniscule proportions. From the mountain tops of God's eternal purposes our troubles become, whatever they are, light and momentary by comparison.

Suffering that is an Inescapable Part of Growth

In 2 Corinthians 6:3–10 NIV Paul links the question of suffering to maturity in ministry and servanthood.

> *'We put no stumbling block in anyone's path, so that our ministry will not be discredited. Rather, as servants of God, we commend ourselves in every way; in great endurance, in troubles, hardships and distresses, in beatings, imprisonments and riots; in hard work, sleepless nights, and hunger; in purity, understanding, patience, and kindness; in the Holy Spirit, and in sincere love, in truthful speech and in the power of God; with*

weapons of righteousness in the right hand and in the left; through glory and dishonor, bad report and good report; genuine yet regarded as imposters; known yet regarded as unknown; dying and yet we live on; beaten and yet not killed; sorrowful yet always rejoicing; poor yet making many rich; having nothing and yet possessing everything.'

Paul is speaking here about growing pains, the suffering and discomfort that is an inescapable, even necessary part of the process of growth. Here are the three principles that are important to see us through these pressures.

Principle 1. In every area, development and growth come only through stretching our capacities to the point where it hurts.

I was speaking recently to a young woman who was telling me about her first experience of running a marathon, all 26 miles of it. She explained that round about the 15 mile mark you hit what she called the 'pain barrier.' When you hit that barrier, either you die by the side of the road or you struggle on and through it. If you get through, you know you are going to finish the race. There are still 10 miles to go and you may not win, but you know you are going to make it all the way to the tape.

Listening to her, I realised that every area of growth has these pain barriers. You cannot develop physically without pain. You push your body to the point where it hurts, then you push it a bit further. You cannot develop your mind without hitting the pain barrier. It hurts to study, to keep your mind on the job, to struggle to remember, to stay awake through boring lectures and to try and follow an abstruse line of reasoning. You cannot build relationships without pain, hurting the other person and being hurt, asking forgiveness and trying all over again, taking the risk of loving and trusting. It is often painful. And God makes it plain you cannot grow spiritually without pain. No discipline, he tells us, is joyful – it hurts. It is only after the pain that it yields its fruit.

We cannot in fact avoid pain, ever. If we refuse the pain of exercise we will end up with the pain of a sick, weak body. If we avoid the pain of study, we end up with the pain of ignorance. If we avoid the pain of building relationships we will experience the pain of loneliness. If we do not accept the pain of spiritual discipline we experience the pain of spiritual failure.

If we cannot avoid pain, then we should gladly accept the pain of growth as good and normal, learning to push through the barriers we will always meet on the path to maturity.

Principle 2. There is a time lag between the pain and the gain.

You do not experience the gain of the pain straight away. What you experience is generally more pain. The second time it is even worse because you are experiencing pain in places that were already hurting.

It is the same principle however, as sowing and reaping. If we sow we will reap, but not in the same season as we sow. Sometimes I wonder why spiritually I seem to be going through a hard or dry time. Then I look back and see that I am merely reaping what I sowed, and forgot about, six months ago. At other times I experience unexpected outpourings of grace and blessing in my life or ministry and cannot equate it with what I am currently doing in my spiritual work. My prayer life is no more than before, my study of the Bible is about the same, but where did all this power and inspiration come from? Sometimes sown in tears and painful stubborn faithfulness six months or a year ago.

Principle 3. Our capacity to stand the pain depends on the attraction of the goals we have in view.

As in everything, Jesus is our supreme example.

> *'Let us fix our eyes on Jesus, the author and perfecter of our faith, who for the joy set before him endured the cross, scorning its shame, and sat down at the right hand of the throne of God. Consider him who endured such opposition from sinful men, so that you will not grow weary and lose heart.'*
>
> Hebrews 12:2–3 NIV

125

If our goals are small, we will rarely be willing to sacrifice much, or endure much pain to get it. 'It is not worth the effort' we say. The bigger and the more compelling the goal, the more we will be willing to endure and the longer we will be willing to persevere to reach it.

Not only does the goal affect our willingness to endure, it also affects our capacity to endure, that is, how much we can stand. So Jacob, we read, served seven years for Rachel, 'but they seemed like only a few days to him because of his love for her.'

Stress Caused by Unresolved Difficulties and Unanswered Prayers

In 2 Corinthians 12:7–10 NIV there is the well-known passage about Paul's thorn in the flesh.

> *'To keep me from becoming conceited because of these surpassingly great revelations, there was given me a thorn in my flesh, a messenger of Satan to torment me. Three times I pleaded with the Lord to take it away from me. But he said to me, "My grace is sufficient for you, for my power is made perfect in weakness." Therefore I will boast all the more gladly about my weaknesses, so that Christ's power may rest on me. That is why, for Christ's sake, I delight in weaknesses, in insults, in hardships, in persecutions, in difficulties. For when I am weak, then I am strong.'*

We are still, after centuries, unclear as to what Paul's thorn in the flesh was. It may have been a sickness, but if so, its nature is unknown. Someone has said you could fill a medical dictionary with the various diagnoses that have been made. It may have been a demonic attack or it may have been a difficult personal adversary, but whatever it was it brought acute stress and suffering into the apostle's life. What is more, it seemed intractable, it did not go and God did not remove it.

The thorn represents for us the stress and suffering that

come into our life when there are difficulties that never seem to get resolved, in spite of all our praying and all our believing. Faith that works for us in other areas of our life somehow does not work in this area. Worse still, faith that works for other people in this selfsame area, we discover does not work for us. We run the whole gamut of emotions from exasperation to anger, to guilt and fear and despair. We are ashamed to let our situation be known because we are supposed to be leaders and we observe people who are under us, or are spiritually less mature than us, who have overcome the very same problem without much difficulty.

But out of his experience, Paul uncovers the principles that will help us handle this particularly excruciating form of stress.

Principle 1. The purpose of the thorn is meant to be known.

The thorn did not drive Paul to rebellion or despair or guilt or confusion. It drove him to entreaty. Three times he pleaded with the Lord and he got a satisfying explanation and one that he was glad to live with. The nature and purpose of the thorn is identified, it has a specific objective and it will only accomplish that purpose when we know what it is and allow it to do its work.

Principle 2. The thorn is a balancing factor.

This is a term that Bob Mumford uses and it catches the point very clearly. Paul understood that the thorn was painful, but it was protective. It was meant to save him from even more serious dangers such as conceit, arrogance and self exaltation because of the magnitude of the revelations that he had received. To keep the great apostle of the Gentiles aware of the fact that he is not superhuman, he is left with the humiliating evidence that he has a problem that he cannot get resolved and a prayer that God repeatedly answers in the negative.

I have seen the balancing factor operating in the lives of many brothers and sisters that God is using greatly and I notice the meekness and the sensible humility it induces. They do not think more highly of themselves than they ought to think, but rather think of themselves with sober judgment. (Romans 12:3) But the first step is always to know what God is doing, only then can we allow him to work without our getting too much in the way.

Principle 3. The thorn teaches the methods of divine power.

Power, God told Paul, is perfected in weakness. But what does that mean? Does God want us to be like limp rag dolls, completely powerless, so that he does everything through us by himself and we move like mere marionettes? Certainly not that, and yet Paul clearly links power and weakness, not only conceptually but experientially. He says, 'When I am weak I am strong.'

I began to get some clarity on this when I realised what is being taught is that man is meant to be a conductor of divine power. I asked a friend of mine who is an electrical engineer, what made one metal a good conductor of power and another metal a poor conductor. His answer was illuminating. A metal is a good conductor, he said, when the electrons in the metal get detached from the metal and flow with the power. In a metal that is a poor conductor, the electrons resist getting detached from the metal to flow with the power.

Men and women are intended to be conductors of divine power but they have an inbuilt resistance to it because that power is power for others. God's grace, in other words, is sufficient for us to live a life of sacrificial self-giving.

> '*So then, death is at work in us, but life is at work in you.*'
> 2 Corinthians 4:12 NIV

> '*So I will very gladly spend for you everything I have and expend myself as well.*'
> 2 Corinthians 12:15 NIV

The purpose of the thorn is to drive us into God and make us receptive to his grace and not resistant to it. It demonstrably did its work in Paul. He wrote his discovery of God's all sufficient grace in 2 Corinthians 9:8 NIV.

> *'And God is able to make all grace abound to you, so that in all things at all times, having all that you need, you will abound in every good work.'*

Where and how did Paul learn that? Through the thorn.

The Son of God has many crowns now, crowns of glory and crowns of life. What is his favourite crown? I suspect it is still the crown of thorns, because there, at the Cross, the supreme manifestation of God's power, it was also supremely death working in him but life working in us.

Chapter 13

Relationships –
The Leader's Network

Another of the things that marks out leaders from mere visionaries is that leaders, even the most task oriented of them, are always inescapably involved with people.

Leaders not only have to have a vision of the future, they must conceptualise their vision into goals.

Leaders must not only conceptualise their goals, they must articulate them and communicate them to other people.

Leaders not only have to share their goals with people, they have to find the ones who are willing to follow them towards the goal.

Furthermore, leaders remain leaders only so long as these conditions are maintained in being. This is particularly the case with organisations such as churches which are based on voluntarism, that is, the people are not generally paid to take on the responsibilities or do the jobs that have to be done. Thus leaders in these organisations cannot rely on the assistance of monetary remuneration to motivate people. Only genuine leadership will produce results and that requires that leaders be involved, not only with plans but with people.

Leaders are involved with the dynamics of relationships in two directions, firstly the relationships between them and their people, and secondly the relationships of their people with each other. Both are vital and both need constant attention and input. And they are interrelated, if the relationships in one direction are strained, then sooner or later relationships in the other direction will deteriorate.

Relationships Between Leaders and People

Leaders have to be constantly tuned in to the quality of the relationship they have with their people, because that is one of the most accurate indicators of the state of morale of the organisation. Moreover, tending to this relationship is one of their chief preoccupations. Vision and goals have to be repeated, reinforced, reaffirmed and rekindled all along the way. People have to be motivated, encouraged, inspired and animated over and over again. And leaders are not entitled to become upset or disillusioned when this becomes necessary, it is an essential part of their function. As we have already seen, the people are not as oriented towards the future as are the leaders, therefore when the going gets rough, present problems appear to them to be far more convincing than future possibilities. But this is exactly when leaders are needed; when things are going smoothly, they appear almost passengers, but in bad times they are the difference between survival and disaster.

If you have any doubts about this being the case, read again the saga of Moses leading Israel from Egypt to Canaan. The Bible records at least 14 occasions of grumbling and rebellion among the people, more than once to the point where they were ready to stone Moses and elect other leaders to take them back to Egypt. And Moses not only had to endure antagonism and discord from his closest associates but at times he faced the resistance and opposition of the entire nation almost singlehandedly. As we know the pressure got too much even for the mildest man that ever lived. In an extremity of irritation Moses smote the rock at Kadesh and forfeited his own right to enter the land.

Relationships Within the Organisation

Leaders must also continually oversee the state of the relationships amongst the people. Leaders who are very task and goal oriented often neglect this maintenance aspect of their function. Either they are blind to the presence of friction or disputes within the ranks, or else they are impatient with what seems to them to be totally childish and irrational behaviour. Ignoring and neglecting such problems can mean that the whole project, or even the whole organisation suddenly disintegrates before the leaders' eyes and they find themselves becoming the target of criticism and hostility from all sides.

At first the trouble may have had little or nothing to do with the leaders as such, but as emotions rise, facts become distorted and positions become more entrenched. When this takes place there is very often a growing feeling that the leaders have failed everybody by letting things get to such a pass. And that feeling is a correct one. The maintenance of unity and cohesiveness in the organisation is an essential part of the leaders' responsibility and one that they neglect at their peril.

On the other hand people-centred leaders may also fail. They can become so involved in maintaining warm, loving relationships that they lose sight of goals altogether. There may be excellent pastoring going on but no real leadership, so that there is a growing realisation that the church or the organisation is not going anywhere. Eventually the more goal-oriented people begin to complain about the lack of purpose, and some of them may even begin to take over leadership by default, causing problems with the official leaders and sometimes themselves adding to the confusion by heading off in all kinds of different directions.

What Are Relationships?

I am convinced that one of the main reasons why we have so many difficulties with relationships is because we assume that they are part of the common stock of knowledge that everybody possesses and that all we need to do is improve our performance here and there. If that were even partly true we would not have the problems we do, because the bulk of them arise from relationships that are not working as they should. We need, in fact, to go back to the beginning and learn the whole business of relationships from the ground up. I have dealt with the whole subject in the book, 'Right Relationships' but some aspects are so crucial to the whole issue of leadership, and so rarely dealt with from that angle that they need specific treatment.

Consider first of all a simple definition of what is involved in inter-personal relationships, leaving out of consideration at the moment any question of man's relationships with his environment or the animal kingdom.

A relationship is the mutual sharing of life between two or more persons.

Certain important implications arise from this ample definition and to these we now turn.

Mutuality

For a relationship to exist at all, both parties have to contribute something to the interaction. Thus in business, employers contribute wages, employees contribute time, skill and energy; in the classroom, teachers contribute knowledge and instruction, pupils contribute their attention and effort and so on. The contribution does not have to be equal on both sides, or of the same kind, but mutuality, that is, something contributed from both sides, has to be there for a relationship to be created.

In the relationship of leaders and people there needs to be clarity and agreement as to the distinctive contribution that is expected from the leaders and from the people. I know broken-hearted leaders who have been rejected or replaced by churches and other organisations to whom they felt they had given everything they had. In many cases, the sad reality was they had given everything except the one thing that was expected of them, and that was leadership. It often occurs because a person who is not a leader is placed in a leadership position. Not only is the leadership that is required not forthcoming, but the person's other valuable gifts and capacities in other directions are frustrated or rejected.

What Leaders Contribute

Whatever else the leaders' role in an organisation may include, it will always embrace the following essential functions which together constitute a virtual Ten Commandments of Leadership. The leaders' distinctive contribution to the organisation is to –

1. Develop and conceptualise the overarching vision or the long term overriding purpose to be achieved.
2. Clarify and articulate goals and objectives.
3. See that the long range plans and the organisational structures that will be needed to enable the organisation to attain its goals are specified.
4. Allocate the responsibilities and determine the accountability for major departments, or segments of the task.
5. Determine the means to be used to monitor results, measure progress and decide the corrective action that may be required.
6. Act as a key resource for solving problems and overcoming difficulties encountered along the way.
7. Communicate goals and objectives and any modifications or changes in direction.
8. Motivate, inspire, encourage and reward effort and achievement; correct and discipline unsatisfactory performance; maintain morale and team spirit.
9. Take final responsibility for results or outcomes, 'the buck stops here.'
10. Represent the group or organisation in its dealings with the wider environment.

What the People Contribute

The people who are following the leaders are also called upon to make a significant contribution towards realising the goals and objectives of the organisation. They provide the time and effort and the operational talents needed to manage the organisation and carry out its detailed, day to day activities.

The demarcation between the kinds of things leaders have to do and the kind of things that others in the organisation do is, of course, not always clear cut. There will inevitably be a certain amount of overlap, depending on the size of the organisation, the nature of the goals and other situational factors. Nevertheless leaders who have not mastered the art of getting things done through other people and who get involved with detail at the expense of the planning and organising that are their primary responsibility will never be effective leaders or will be effective only with small teams or projects.

Blame for Breakdown

The aspect of mutuality also means that if a relationship breaks down there has always been failure on both sides, either wrong actions or wrong reactions or both. Never is all the fault on one side and total innocence on the other. Therefore wherever there are leaders who have failed their people, there are also people who have failed their leaders. We are weak at recognising our corporate responsibility in this regard which is perhaps one of the chief reasons why the church has such a poor record in dealing with and rescuing leaders who fail.

Reconciliation

Furthermore if a relationship breaks down, reconciliation can never be unilateral, both parties have to do something to bridge the divide.

Again, when there has been a breakdown between leaders and people the prospect of reconciliation is often ruined by the tendency for a church or fellowship to split and for individuals and groups affected by the situation to go their own ways. This may be an understandable way out of a difficult situation but it surely has often to be seen as failure and the premature closing of the door to the possibility of reconciliation and restoration.

The Relationship – A Separate Factor

It is important to realise that when a relationship comes into being, the relationship itself becomes a separate factor alongside the parties who make it up. The relationship is not independent of the parties because without the parties there is no relationship, nevertheless it is a distinct factor that has to be given attention and tended to on its own merits.

This is commonly recognised in the business world where the employer/employee relationship is usually prescribed very carefully in a job description, conditions of employment or union award. In more informal and in more intimate relationships the distinction between the persons and the relationship between them is often blurred and this blurring becomes a fruitful source of problems.

Some groups, for example, attempt to create unity and community by trying to level out individual quirks and differences almost as though people will be able to function harmoniously with one another only if they are all a standard pattern. The results are uniformly disastrous. Community is created only by working on the relationships as relationships; individuality is therefore not only to be admitted, it is to be welcomed, it is not only to be accommodated, it is to be encouraged. Community is the integration of individuality and the way we integrate it is through relationships.

It is because relationships are a separate factor that you often find such a disparity between the individuals who make up a group and its team spirit or esprit de corps. One group has leaders and people, with outstanding personal abilities but they remain a bunch of individualists who accomplish very little as a team. Another comprises quite ordinary leaders and people of very mediocre talents, but they are knit into a cohesive unit with extraordinary vitality and effectiveness. The difference is that the individuals in the latter group are putting everything they have into team work, that is, in relationships, while those in the former group are putting very little of what they have into the team.

Describing Relationships

We spend our lives involved in relationships of so many kinds that we need some categories that can be used to describe them in a way that reduces the complexity. There are four that will be found generally useful.

The first two describe the broad classes of relationships and the last two describe essential characteristics.

1. Classes of relationships.
(a) Instrumental or co-operative
(b) Social or consummatory

2. Characteristics of relationships.
(a) Intimacy or closeness
(a) Scope or extent

Instrumental or Co-operative Relationships

These relationships have their origin in the creation mandate in Genesis 1:28 when God gave humankind authority over the created order. The essential nature of these relationships is that they are instruments, that is they are the means to do something. Individuals enter into cooperative relationships to undertake a common task or achieve a common purpose. The relationships thus formed are therefore a means to an end and without the existence of that goal or purpose there would be nothing to cause the people to form the relationship.

The great majority of the relationships we form are of this type – employer/employee, pupil/teacher, supplier/customer and doctor/patient. All of these are built around the achievement of a task or goal or purpose; once the task is finished, or it is clear that the goal cannot be achieved, the relationships that depended on them cease.

It follows that in instrumental relationships the primary emphasis tends to be placed on the task or the purpose because the relationships are in being to serve that end.

Consummatory or Social Relationships

In Genesis 2:18 we have something quite different, God's creation of woman because it was 'not good' for man to be alone. Here we have the beginning of all those relationships which are social rather than vocational. We call them consummatory because they are not a means to an end but an end in themselves. They are 'good' in themselves in that they need no external goal or purpose to justify their existence. We enter into such relationships for the sake of the relationship, not for anything the relationship can enable us to do.

Marriage is the first example of a consummatory relationship, friendships are another. If I say to someone, 'I would really like to be your friend' and they say 'What for?', I understand that they have missed the whole point of the relationship.

Few relationships of course, are purely instrumental or purely consummatory. Not only does work have important social aspects but families and friends sometimes join forces for specific projects. Nevertheless in the latter case, the task does not create the relationship which was there before the task began and will still be there after the task is finished.

Misunderstanding the Relationship

Because of the mixed nature of most relationships it is possible for people to have differing understandings of the essential character of the interaction. This is a very fruitful source of problems.

For example if I find my friendship is being cultivated because I could be a good support at the committee table for the other person's project, I will feel I am being 'used'. Friendship is not meant to be a means to an end, in my book at any rate. On the other hand if a salesman calls at my office and then settles down for a cosy chat about his family and his weekend activities I am likely to get irritated because he is 'wasting my time.' He is there for a task and ought to get on with it.

But I would see nothing wrong with a colleague lobbying for my support for a project, or with a friend dropping by the office for a chat. In these cases the nature of the relationship is understood and respected on both sides and there is no sense of it being misused for other ends.

The same distinction requires that people cannot reasonably expect the foreman or manager to treat them as a buddy and be sensitive to their every need. They must abide by the general terms of the relationship which is primarily an instrumental one and not take it amiss if the emphasis is on quality and productivity and not on social interaction.

Here Are Some of the Problems That Can Arise

1. The task or project oriented house group leader who complains about one or two of the members of the group who are 'uncommitted'. They come only when they feel like it and are hard to pin down when it comes to participation in the programme. The chances are that the heart of the problem is that the leader unconsciously looks on relationships in the house group as basically instrumental. They exist so that there is good fellowship in the group, effective prayer times, profitable bible study and fruitful outreach. That is what the house church is 'for'.

On the other hand the hang loose people may unconsciously view the relationships in the house group as consummatory. They go to house group when they feel like going because they do not go 'for' bible study, or 'for' prayer or 'for' anything, they just go for the sake of being part of the home group.

2. The leader who operates on the principle of 'management by exception' that is, you need to manage only the things that are not functioning properly; things that are working well don't need your time or input. This leader therefore gives his attention to the people or the activities that are having problems. In ancient wisdom, the squeaking axle gets the grease. But what can happen is that the faithful, consistent workers begin to feel unappreciated, or some of them begin to develop problems because then they get at least some attention from the leaders.

3. Very people-oriented leaders tend to value the

relationships within the group for the sake of the relationships. Therefore they are reluctant to challenge, confront, extend or disturb people or to stir them out of their pleasant cosiness. The group becomes a nice, warm, comfortable, introverted huddle that is going nowhere and to the leaders' surprise eventually dies of boredom because there is no challenge or direction.

4. Sometimes people employed in a Christian business become discontented because they feel there is not enough prayer or Bible study or time for fellowship in the office. All of these things are important no doubt, but they are not the primary reason for that work relationship.

In Christian communities and missions the position is further complicated in that relationships between the members can vary within the course of a single day. For example, at one time I am clearly a subordinate and somebody is my manager for that particular task. Out of work hours however we are merely brothers and sisters together, but in the evening Bible study, I am the leader and teacher and my erstwhile boss is now one of my students.

Intimacy or Closeness

The question of intimacy in personal relationships can be something of a minefield because the greater the intimacy the more highly charged the emotional field is likely to be. Furthermore, the parties to the relationship often have very different expectations as to the level of intimacy that is appropriate but these views are rarely expressed. Blundering around in an uncharted minefield is not to be recommended.

If people expect more personal intimacy from the leaders than the leaders provide, the latter will be regarded as 'standoffish' or aloof. If the leaders seek greater intimacy with people than the people expect or want, they run the risk of being regarded as intrusive or inquisitive.

The position is often particularly sensitive when it comes to personal friendships between church leaders and individual members in the church.

From those not admitted to this intimacy, but who would like to be, there are often accusations of an 'in-group', or 'the favoured few', whose views get preferential treatment and so on. Jealousy and envy flourish.

Leaders are therefore generally advised not to have personal friends amongst their congregation because such friendships cause problems. The result is great loneliness amongst Christian leaders that is often a major contributory factor in leadership failure and burnout. I fear some have almost lost the capacity for friendship altogether so that they cannot be friends even with other leaders. And if leaders do not know how to be friends, how can they model that relationship before their people? How can you produce a friendly church with leaders who have no friends anywhere in sight?

It is not necessary for leaders to be caught in either dilemma. Sensible principles for handling relationships between leaders and people need to be established and clearly taught until they are naturally accepted as the norm. Nor is this unknown. For example the rules of the first Moravian community in Herrenhut, established by Count Zinzendorf in 1722 stated explicitly that the elders of the community were entitled to have their own personal friends and no one must take it amiss if they saw others more intimate with the elders than they were. Such astonishing commonsense needs to be relearned in many churches and church organisations today.

It necessitates, of course, that we distinguish very clearly between friendship and favouritism. Because I have a special place with one of the leaders as his or her personal friend it does not mean that I have privileges over others in any other aspect of community life. Leaders have to guard against that for the sake of friendship as well as for the sake of the community. When an opening for advancement or responsibility comes along friends must not have, and must not seem to have a head start over others.

> *'What will you say when he appoints over you,*
> *And you yourself had taught them –*
> *Former companions to be over you?'* Jeremiah 13:21 ASB

This is not an impossible ideal. It can work very successfully and very naturally and certainly much more easily in the context of team leadership.

There is another aspect that needs to be understood. Intimacy is the end result of a whole range of factors including compatability of temperament, common goals, shared interests and mutual attraction. This means that we cannot be equally intimate with everybody, nor should we expect others to be with us. Even Jesus had two groups of disciples, the 70 and the 12. He was much more intimate with the 12 than he was with the 70. And amongst the 12 there were three, Peter, James and John with whom he was especially close. He took them with him into places where the others did not come. And of the three, John 'the disciple who lay on Jesus' bosom' had a special place.

In some sections of the church, particularly those who have experienced renewal, intimacy and commitment are often confused, as though commitment is only possible to those with whom we are very intimate. Therefore only two types of relationship are modelled, the very close, intimate type (committed) and the distant, emotionally uninvolved type (uncommitted). This is dangerously inadequate. It is possible, and I know because I experience them, to have deeply committed relationships with people without a high level of intimacy, and for those relationships to be valid and valuable. Sometimes by their very distance they can be more disinterested and objective than others that are emotionally closer. There is a great need, and a great opportunity in the church today, to model a far greater range of valid, worthwhile, healthy and fulfilling relationships than we have yet attempted.

Scope or Extent

We also face the question of scope, that is how much of my life is meant to be involved in this particular relationship. As with intimacy, problems occur when the parties to a relationship have differing understanding or expectancies but these are never expressed. For example, a manager who considers that his relationship with his staff starts at 8 am and finishes at 5 pm may well feel that what a worker does in his own time or his private life is none of his business. But the message his staff may read into it is that he is insensitive and not interested in their family problems. 'Sort these things out in your own time but don't let them interfere with your work.' On the other hand the foreman or manager who is interested in his staff to the extent that he likes to be invited to the barbecue or asks after their weekend activities may be seen as intrusive by those of his staff who think that their relationship with him goes no further than the factory gates or the office door.

The question of scope or extent emphasises that every relationship has boundaries and these must be known and clearly understood by all concerned. Leaders in particular need to know where the leader/people relationship ends and where the person's private life begins because regardless of the nature of the relationship, there are areas of personal privacy and responsibility that no one is entitled to intrude into without invitation or without the right to enter having been freely given by the person concerned.

It is, of course, much easier to concede that there are limits to a relationship than to define exactly where the boundaries lie. This is especially the case in Christian organisations where leadership and ministry roles that have quite different functions may be filled by the same person. It may be difficult in such situations to prescribe the line of demarcation but it is still essential to do so.

For example, I may be a leader in a church and also be involved in its counselling ministry. The authority I have to speak into the private lives of those who come to me for counsel is quite different from my right to speak into the private lives of those who are under my leadership but have not sought my counselling assistance. On the other hand, in my leadership function it may be appropriate for me to determine and direct the corporate activities of people in a way that would be quite wrong for me to do as a counsellor.

The Building Blocks of Relationships

We come now to the elements or factors that are necessary to build relationships and to maintain them in life and health. Mutual participation there must be, but of itself that is not enough. The same can be said of having a common interest or a joint purpose. Important as these are, they are not sufficient on their own to guarantee the success, let alone the survival of a relationship. Many marriages, business partnerships or missions start out with all of these but peter out or blow apart further down the track.

All relationships consist of four elements that constitute the basic building blocks. Other things may be involved, may even be important, but these four are essential. If any of them are neglected or adversely affected, the relationship will come under stress. If the failure is not addressed or corrected, the relationship will begin to break down.

The four factors we will examine are:

1. Trust, the most fragile of the four.
2. Love, the most rugged and enduring.
3. Respect or honour, the most neglected, and
4. Understanding or knowledge, the one that takes longest.

The relative importance of these factors may vary from one relationship to the next, so may the specific ways in which they are expressed. Nevertheless all four are essential in every relationship and none can be neglected without serious consequences. Furthermore they cannot substitute for each other. You cannot say I love my people but I don't understand them all that well and I can't really trust them. Love will not carry the whole burden. Relationships were made to stand solidly on all four legs; if one is weak they will wobble, if two go, they will undoubtedly collapse. To build enduring relationships we need to know what we have to do in each of the four areas, and to these we turn in the next chapters.

Chapter 14

Trust, the Cost of Commitment

Of all the elements of relationships, the one that is most crucial to leadership is probably trust. Generally speaking, the more important the relationship, the more vital is the part played by trust. If I am dangling over a cliff on the end of a rope, the thing uppermost in my mind regarding the man on the other end of the rope is not whether I like him but whether I can trust him. Similarly, the more important the relationship is, the more costly the commitment of real trust becomes, because the more there is at stake.

Leadership is a position of trust, and in any position of trust the greater burden of responsibility rests on the party that has most power. Leaders always have more power than others because the leaders control all the most important decisions and have more knowledge than other people as to what is going on. Here as elsewhere, knowledge is power, which is why leaders generally like to control the amount and timing of information releases. The message they often convey to their people by such a policy however, is that they do not trust them.

What is Trust?

Because it is so important to leadership relationships, we need to understand just what trust is and why we seem to have perennial difficulties with it, both in our relationship with God and our relationships with each other.

1. Trust is a choice we make.
We cannot be forced to trust: if we do it, we must do it voluntarily. Therefore if leaders say 'You will just have to trust us in this step' people will always resent it, and will feel trapped. One thing you can be sure of is that trust will not be created.

2. Trust is a risk we take.
The risk we take in trusting is that we thereby let some part of our life go out of our control and into the hands of somebody else because the outcome of that particular issue now depends on the person or the people we have trusted. The cost involved in trust is that we have thereby accepted a position of vulnerability because we are no longer in control of that part of our destiny, whether the part is great or small. When people trust leaders they often let outcomes affecting very important areas of their lives go out of their control and into the hands of the leaders, and the vulnerability that ensues can be a very frightening thing. Few leaders appreciate the cost of the trust they sometimes expect as of right from their people.

3. The evidence that we have trusted is that we have made no contingency plans in case we are let down.
If I say that I trust you but then arrange a back up or a fall back position in case you let me down, what I am communicating is that I do not really trust you at all, or that I am putting you to the test to see if I can trust you.

4. Because trust involves vulnerability, strong emotions are always aroused when trust is broken, particularly when it is broken by leaders.
The effect of a breach of trust is that part of our universe that we thought was safe and dependable is suddenly found to be uncertain and unpredictable. The emotions likely to be aroused by this dangerous discovery are fear and anxiety and

the normal defensive response to fear is anger. Leaders who have been involved in some failure that has lost them the trust of their people are invariably startled and dismayed at the amount of emotion generated and the anger often displayed towards them. They need to understand the reason for it.

5. There is a necessary link between trust and responsibility or accountability.

When people trust leaders they let certain outcomes go out of their control and into the control of the leaders, which means that the leaders are then answerable for those outcomes and accountable for any failure. One of the marks of a leader is the ability and the willingness to shoulder responsibility for results.

The question then is, to whom are leaders responsible or accountable? The answer is that they are responsible and accountable to the people who have trusted them. Thus, while they may be responsible to people above them, they are also responsible to people below them. Many Christian leaders do not understand this, and some would dispute it, but trust necessarily creates accountability and neglect of that principle has caused devastation in some situations. Authority not only flows from the top down, it is given from the bottom up, even in the case of political rulers, as is demonstrated in the case of Reheboam the son of Solomon.

> 'When all Israel saw that the king refused to listen to them, they answered the king:
> *"What share do we have in David,*
> *What part in Jesse's son?*
> *To your tents O Israel!*
> *Look after your own house, O David!"'* 1 Kings 12:17 NIV

6. Trust is fragile, and once broken, is very difficult to restore.

Forgiveness is the work of a moment but the restoration of trust is something different, it is very, very difficult and it always takes time. This is something that leaders and others who are guilty of breach of trust, often do not realise until too late.

What Are They Trusting?

Because of its importance to leadership we have to take the discussion a stage further and ask what it is in their leaders that the people are actually trusting. Unless we know what it is, we may unwittingly break trust or be accused of breaking trust and not understand why. Whether people consciously think of it in these terms or not, the following are qualities they are putting their confidence in.

1. The judgment of the leaders.
People have to trust the judgment of their leaders simply because they cannot see the future, or see the goals, as clearly as the leaders can. Therefore they are following, trusting that the leaders have got the goals right and that they have got the right goals.

People are trusting the leaders' judgment, not their persuasiveness which is why it is always harder to trust new or untried leaders, because there is no track record to go on. As leaders demonstrate the reliability of their judgment, the people's confidence in them will grow.

Changes in leadership are generally times of stress for an organisation because trust has to be transferred from leaders whose judgment people have learned to depend on, to leaders the quality of whose judgment they still have to discover. Ideally, from the point of view of confidence, new leadership should grow up from within the organisation so that there is a natural succession as there was from Moses to Joshua.

> *'Now Joshua son of Nun was filled with the spirit of wisdom because Moses had laid his hands on him. So the Israelites listened to him and did what the Lord commanded Moses.'*
> Deuteronomy 34:9 NIV

> *'That day the Lord exalted Joshua in the sight of all Israel and they revered him all the days of his life, just as they had revered Moses.'*
> Joshua 4:14 NIV

Because people have to trust the leaders' judgment it follows that when leaders are communicating decisions, they should always make clear the basis for their judgment, that is, the certainties, the probabilities, the assumptions or estimates and the faith steps. We have already dealt with this in the context of communicating vision, but its implications in terms of trust need also to be emphasised.

2. The resourcefulness of the leaders.

People are also trusting that the leaders have the resourcefulness to handle the unknown future and the ability to find answers to problems and meet contingencies as and when they arise. Here also, confidence in leaders grows as they demonstrate their competence in handling difficulties and problems. It is impossible to eliminate all uncertainty and risk as far as the future is concerned but one of the tasks of leadership is to try and reduce that uncertainty to manageable proportions. Forecasting, budgeting, estimating and forward planning all have this aim in view.

But the people's confidence in the ability of their leaders to handle the unknown future is also a reflection of the leaders' inner confidence in themselves – or their lack of it.

If the leaders of an organisation do not have that inner confidence you will often detect a sense of uneasiness and disquiet in the people, even when things are going well. On the other hand where leaders do have confidence you will find an air of buoyancy and optimism amongst the people even if things are going badly. But leaders' confidence must be real, people can usually tell when the leaders are merely putting on a bold front or saying positive things to cover up their uncertainty.

3. Trusting the leaders' perseverance.

People are also trusting that their leaders will stick with the vision until they actually reach their goal or will stay with the project until it is finished. Leaders do not, in most people's view, have the luxury of opting out or losing heart if the going gets rough. Their perceived role is to hang in there and keep the vessel on course when everybody else is ready to give up and abandon ship. Moreover, leaders are not to look for any special praise or kudos for doing the job in these circumstances because that is what leaders are for.

There are some leaders who seek to hand the reins over to someone else or discover a 'call' to another place if they suspect that the present project could go under. They do not want their reputation tarnished by failure. If people suspect this is likely they will never feel secure when difficulties occur, and they will always feel betrayed by leaders who get out while the going is good and leave somebody eles to face the music.

Other leaders shine best in hopeless circumstances because then there is nothing more to lose, little is expected of them and anything achieved is a plus. Such leaders may feel less secure on the upswing because now everybody expects them to succeed, so anything they achieve will be taken for granted while failure or even only partial success could be a disgrace.

Closely linked to perseverance is the question of character or moral fibre, that is, the ability of leaders to stand up under pressure and stress. Remember that a crisis never creates character, all it does is reveal the character that is already there. People can be very perceptive in reading this aspect of a person's character and if they suspect that the leaders would buckle under pressure or do unethical things to get off the hook, they will always feel unsafe, even in good times. Something like this undoubtedly lies behind the attention given to character as a qualifier for leadership in the early church.

4. The integrity of the leaders.
I learned a very important lesson on this aspect of leadership in the early 1960's when we were involved in some of the very first Catholic charismatic prayer meetings in New Zealand. Those dear Catholic saints knew so little in those early days, that they believed almost everything I told them – very flattering, and very dangerous. Then one time I shared with them something I really thought I had from God, only to find to my dismay during the next week that I had got it all wrong. I spent a couple

of sleepless nights over it, thinking, 'If I tell them what has happened they'll never believe me again.' But I remembered something a friend of mine had said years before, 'If you make a mistake and don't admit it, you end up defending a lie and lay yourself open to deception.'

So next meeting I said, 'Last week I told you such and such and I really thought I had it from God. The simple fact is – I was wrong. Please forget what I said and forgive me for my blunder.' It didn't of course come out as smoothly as that – but do you know what I discovered? From that point on they really began to trust me. People do not expect their leaders to be infallible, although some leaders think they are meant to be, but they do expect them to be honest. They will follow you almost anywhere as long as they are sure that if you make a mistake and lead them into danger, you will admit it and lead them back to safe ground. If they are not sure of that, they will not follow you very far, nor should they. I wouldn't. Such leaders may get it right 19 times in a row and the 20th time lead everybody into a disaster simply because they are too proud, or too insecure to admit to having made a mistake.

Leaders need to be very frank and very honest about mistakes, without making excuses, evading responsibility or rationalising. Rationalising is giving a reason that is not the real reason but is one that is more acceptable to our self image. It is an unconscious defence mechanism to save us from unpleasant ego insights. It is often easier for an individual to rationalise than for a group, because, in a group, there is usually someone who will explode the myth by saying 'Hang it all, that's not the real reason. If we are going to give the people this story let's be honest and admit we are deceiving them.'

Leaders Have to Trust Their People

Like all aspects of relationships, trust has to be mutual, it has to operate from both sides. Not only do people have to trust their leaders, but leaders have to trust their people. Here I detect a great area of failure on the part of many Christian leaders, they do not seem to have a lot of faith in their people. But if leaders do not really trust their people they must not be surprised if that lack of trust is reciprocated. Because leaders are accustomed to being in charge of things, it is not easy for them to let things go out of their control. This is why it is usually very difficult to lead leaders.

In any organisation, including churches and Christian communities, where the leaders have reserved to themselves the final exercise of power or the final authority to make decisions, just in case things go wrong I suspect there is at bottom a lack of trust; the leaders do not trust their people to be as wise or as just or as intelligent or as holy as they are.

How to Build Trust

When we examine the matter of trust in relationships we find that, like faith in the New Testament, to which it is close kin, trust is both a crisis and a process. There is a point at which we make a decision or take an action that constitutes a commitment of trust, but one act of trust is not enough, it is also something that develops gradually. In fact, the New Testament has more to say about building faith after we have trusted Christ than about how to make the initial commitment in the first place.

Trust as decision

As interaction takes place between people there is often a period of exploration or uncertainty as to whether a real relationship will emerge or not. But ultimately there is a point of decision where one either commits oneself or not. Up to that point, swings of 'for' or 'against', 'yes' or 'no' are perfectly appropriate. But after the decision point, to change one's mind or revert to uncertainty is already disloyalty.

The same applies with leadership. Since churches and similar groups are voluntary associations, a vote to call or appoint certain leaders may guarantee them a position, but does not ensure that they have the trust of all the people. But if the relationship is ever to succeed there must come a point where the people as a whole decide to commit themselves to the leaders and the leaders commit themselves to the people. Only then is true trust involved because a heart commitment has been made, and only after that is it possible to speak of loyalty and disloyalty.

In this type of commitment, I believe the initiative ought always to come from the leaders. They must commit themselves to the people before they can expect a committed response. In this, as in everything, they are to lead. Many relationships start off on the wrong foot because leaders wait for commitment before they commit themselves. Trust does not just happen, ultimately you have to do it.

Trust as process
Nevertheless one act of trust is not enough, trust is a progressive thing, it has to be developed but probably our biggest gap in teaching relational skills is lack of instruction on how to build trust.

First of all, note the difference between trusting someone and putting them to the test or trying them out to see if they can be trusted. There is a legitimate place for both but we must always make it clear which it is we are doing. If I say I am trusting you to do this job properly and you fail, the message is that you have let me down and shown that you cannot be trusted. But if I say, I am giving you a chance to show whether you can do this job or not, the situation is quite different. If you fail, all that has been demonstrated is that either I made a mistake in giving you the job or you made a mistake in taking it on. The fragile plant of trust has not been damaged.

Building Trustworthiness

It is a major task for leaders to build trustworthiness in their people, as it is for parents to build trustworthiness in their children. How is this to be done? Here are some suggestions.

1. Be prepared to take risks.
There is no costless trust and if we are going to build trust-worthiness in people we can only do it by taking real risks with them and making real acts of trust.

2. Play to their strengths, not their weaknesses.
Begin by trusting them with things that they are good at and can do well. Your aim is to help them to succeed every time, therefore weight the scales in their favour at the start.

3. Build trust gradually.
The principle is 'Line on line, a little here, a little there.' Remember you are building trust, not trying to find out how far you can trust.

4. Express your confidence in them and in their progress.
Trustworthiness grows by being recognised and every recognition gives the person a stake in protecting that reputation.

5. If they fail, give them another chance.
And be very cautious about expressing lack of trust even if you have been let down. Remember that trust is a very fragile plant. And never say 'I trusted you and you let me down' if you did not make it clear beforehand that a matter of trust was involved.

6. Give them the opportunities and the rewarding responsibilities that their trustworthiness merits.
That is the chief recompense and recognition that trustworthy people seek.

Building Others' Trust In Us

An equally important task for leaders is that of building the people's trust in them. What often makes it temperamentally difficult for leaders to do so is that a climate of trustworthiness is created in very ordinary and very unspectacular ways. Panache and flair are conspicuous by their absence. Note the following important factors.

1. Dependability.
For leaders that means:

(a) Being reliable and conscientious in the discharge of our responsibilities. This does not mean that leaders have to be involved in detail, or administration, almost certainly we ought not to be; but in the responsibilities we do carry it should be a matter of conscience with us to do them well.
(b) Keeping promises, particularly in small things, and where it is at some cost or inconvenience for us to do so. It is only when our undertakings in small things can be trusted that our undertakings in large matters will carry assurance or certainty.
(c) Being consistent, both in actions and moods. People trust leaders who act out of known principles and not out of whim or impulse. Moodiness is emotional inconsistency; it is very difficult to trust someone whose emotional reactions are unpredictable.
(d) Keeping confidences so that sensitive matters entrusted to us are in safe keeping. But never promise to keep something in confidence before you have heard what it is.

2. Honesty.
It is essential that the leaders' word can be relied on. Therefore do not dress up the message in different ways for different people and avoid particularly the evasion of telling only part of the truth so that you can never actually be accused of lying.

3. Loyalty.
Leaders expect their people to be loyal to them, but not many reflect on what loyalty on their part towards their people requires. To be loyal means –

(a) I will be there in the bad times as well as the good.
(b) I will be for you even if everyone else is against you.
(c) I will defend you even at cost or risk to myself.

4. Character.

Leaders always have to work at their character because it is exposed to public scrutiny more than others and will be tested more than others. We must –

(a) Know the weaknesses that have to be strengthened, and guarded against.
(b) Not allow ourselves in our personal lives to take the easy options, remembering that most often the difficult courses of action are the right ones.
(c) Above all, never compromise our principles under external pressure or for the sake of expediency.

5. Fairness.

Leaders must be just and equitable in their dealings with people, avoiding favouritism, partiality and discrimination. We will never be able to completely avoid bias and prejudice but we should be willing to recognise it when it is pointed out and make amends. When we find that we have wronged someone we should acknowledge it readily and seek forgiveness.

6. Capability.

Leaders must be able to demonstrate their ability and resourcefulness, particularly in tackling problems and difficulties without losing their nerve or courage. And don't claim competence and ability beyond what you know you have. You will never lose face by saying, 'I've never done this before, and I don't know if I can but I'll give it my best shot.'

7. Cheerfulness.

Leaders must avoid complaining during the bad times or grumbling when the going gets rough. Remember that nobody forced you to become a leader, and keeping up morale in the bad times is part of your responsibilities.

8. Finally –
Leaders must have confidence. They need confidence in God, in their calling to leadership, and as part of that calling, the ability to find within themselves and in their personal spiritual walk, the resources of courage, faith or hope, that they and their people will need.

Things That Damage Trust

When leaders fail in discharging their leadership responsibilities a breach of trust may be involved. This is not to suggest that leaders must succeed in everything they do or that the smallest error of judgment on their part is a breach of trust. It is simply to observe the reality that people have trusted their leaders to fulfil certain specific responsibilities and repeated failures to do so will damage or destroy that trust. Even if the leaders act in good faith what they do may still be so unsuccessful or inept that people will no longer trust their leadership no matter how convinced they are of their honesty or sincerity. This is dealt with in more detail in chapter 20 'When Leaders Fail.'

1. Breach of confidence.
Few things are more destructive of trust in a relationship than to find that something shared in confidence is now common knowledge. Leaders because of their position often have access to knowledge and information that needs to be kept in confidence, or they are privy to highly personal matters in the lives of people that should not be talked about. Three useful principles may help to reduce the risk of breaches of confidence.

(a) Always make sure, even at the risk of seeming pedantic, that the level of confidentiality is mutually known and understood by all parties. Problems generally arise because the person giving the information thinks it is understood to be confidential and the person receiving the information thinks it is for public consumption – or vice versa.

(b) If you have received something in confidence, be meticulous in keeping the promise you made, do not pass it on unless you get a specific release from the originator.

(c) Never promise to keep something confidential without knowing first what it is, and never get your hands tied so that you have to keep confidence about something said about a third party. In fact one of the rules of the Moravian community was that if you heard something said about a third party who was not present you were obligated to go to the third party and tell him or her what was said!

2. Disloyalty or betrayal.

Disloyalty means, 'In the bad times you weren't there as you promised,' or 'You took sides against me.' Betrayal is even more hurtful, it means, 'You did it for your own personal gain or profit.' That is what distinguishes the actions of Peter and Judas, Peter was disloyal, he denied Jesus out of fear, Judas sold him for 30 pieces of silver. People who are blamed by their leaders before other people when things go wrong are the victims of disloyalty, but people who loyally follow their leaders in a costly stand for principle and then find the leaders abandoning those principles for the sake of a better opportunity feel betrayed.

3. Dishonesty.

Dishonesty in all its forms is highly destructive of trust. How can I trust someone if I cannot be sure that what they tell me is the truth or that they will not cheat or take an unfair advantage of me. What bedevils most of our industrial relationships and societal negotiations is that they too often start from a basic presupposition that the other party cannot be trusted.

One of the commonest ways we are dishonest, and yet seem to get away with it, is making promises and not keeping them. Situational ethics too often gives us a way out. We rationalise that because the circumstances have changed the promise no longer applies. Because of that, most promises today are only provisional. They mean 'As long as it is still convenient,' or 'as long as I still feel the same,' or 'as long as something more important doesn't come up – I promise.' Under these circumstances it is no wonder that commitment tends to be provisional also.

Chapter 15

Who Cares? Love and Leadership

In the biblical understanding of leadership, one of the primary images is that of the leader as shepherd. This is supremely exemplified in David the shepherd-king but it goes back to Moses who prayed for a successor to lead Israel, *'so the Lord's people will not be like sheep without a shepherd.'* (Numbers 27:17 NIV) Micaiah in prophesying the defeat of Israel and Judah at Ramoth-Gilead makes the same link

> *'I saw all Israel scattered on the hills like sheep without a shepherd, and the Lord said "These people have no master"'*
>
> 1 Kings 22:17 NIV

The emphasis is clear. Just as the shepherd is there for the sake of the sheep, so the leader is there for the sake of the people, not the other way around. The Good Shepherd, Jesus says, is the One who lays down his life for the sheep. (John 10:11)

The other important biblical image is that of the leader as father. In the Old Testament Moses is the chief example, leading the rambunctious, rebellious, erratic nation of slaves through the wildnerness, 'as a nursing father carries his infant.' In both Old and New Testaments the leaders of the community were the elders, fathers of families. In the apostolic times they had to first prove their capacity to lead and care for their families before they were qualified to take care of the church. In harmony with this image Paul claims fathering as the term to describe his own personal leadership role amongst the Corinthian church.

> *'Even though you have ten thousand guardians in Christ, you do not have many fathers, for in Christ Jesus I became your father through the gospel.'*   1 Corinthians 4:15 NIV

What is described in both these models is the antithesis of the hard driving, ambitious, task oriented leaders who use people as pawns or means to achieve their goals or further their ambitions. The element that comes to the surface is leadership founded on love.

The one thing that power cannot command is love. Only a true servant leader can be loved because the genuine caring love the leader shows for the people evokes their love in return. One of the many impressive characteristics of David as a leader was his capacity to inspire that kind of devotion from his men, even from the Philistine Ittai who declared;

> *'As surely as the Lord lives, and as my lord the king lives, wherever my lord the king may be, whether it means life or death, there will your servant be.'*   2 Samuel 15:21 NIV

What is Love?

It is not a waste of time to ask the meaning of love because today the word has become so depreciated that it has lost almost all content. It almost needs to be retired until it regains some significance. We love God, we 'love' the music of Mozart or Vivaldi, we 'make' love and we are supposed to love our enemies. One of the problems in English is that we use it as an omnibus kind of word whose meaning is inferred only from the context of our remarks or the setting in which they are spoken. Let us examine some alternative terms that help to give it content particularly in considering the relationships between leaders and followers.

Care – Love in Action

There are two main kinds of love, emotional love which is love of the feelings, and volitional love which is love of the will. Care is essentially the latter, it is love in action. The complaint so often heard in relationships that are supposed to be loving ones is 'You don't care' or about a church community or a business, 'Nobody cares around here.' Usually that is exactly what is wrong.

Care is the litmus paper test for the presence of love and underlines the pervasiveness of our need for it. It is love at its widest reach; nurses who care for their patients, schools that care about their pupils, local councils that care about their districts. No enterprise will ever succeed that does not care for its customers and care for its workers. In business, service is the name of the game, but service is care, for quality, for value, for reliability, for punctuality. It is love in action, attentive to the other person's welfare and concerned for his interests. Mutual care leads to harmony and fruitful interaction. Whenever it is neglected or we become care-less, the result is strife, contention and inefficiency.

The care of leaders for their people is like neighbour love. It is not a matter of our having warm affectionate feelings for them it is a matter of attending to their best interests as faithfully and as consistently as we care for our own. God said to the leaders of Israel in Ezekiel's day, who had misused their position as shepherds –

> *'I will feed my sheep and I will cause them to lie down, says the Lord God. I will seek that which was lost and that which was driven away I will bring again. And I will bind up that which was broken and I will strengthen that which was weak, and that which was fat and strong I will preserve; and I will feed them in judgment.'* Ezekiel 34:15–16 (Douay)

The Content of Care

Leaders' care for their people will therefore include concern for issues such as the following:

1. They have proper facilities, equipment and training to enable them to do the tasks for which they are responsible, and that care is taken for their health, welfare and wellbeing.
2. Every endeavour is made to match the job to the person's gifts and strengths so that work becomes a fulfilling occupation from which they can gain satisfaction.
3. Each person is given active encouragement, opportunity and assistance to develop his or her potential for personal growth and to advance in their chosen career or occupation.
4. Personal interests and needs are not sacrificed to corporate or organisational goals or ends.
5. Each person has the opportunity to engage in work that will provide for their financial needs and that adequately rewards effort and skill.
6. When any person needs help, they can expect an understanding, compassionate and practical response from their leaders.

Kindness – Love and Fellow Feeling

Kindness has its roots in our sense of kinship or fellow feeling. When we are kind to somebody, there is an implicit recognition that in the same circumstances we would want somebody to do the same for us. Therefore what we do is gratuitous and freely done. Unkindness is hurtful precisely because it wounds or breaches this sense of kinship between us.

Leaders sometimes move in different circles to their people, they relate to other leaders or attend meetings others do not have access to. Leaders are also often involved in correcting mistakes or reproving errors. All these things can subtly erode the sense of kinship with their people so that leaders act unkindly without being aware of doing so. But that need not be the case. Reprimand or discipline can be severe without being unkind provided it retains its essential quality of fellow feeling, that is, the attitude that in similar circumstances this is the very thing we would want somebody to do for us. We are speaking here of attitudes. If the leader is a kindly person, that kindliness will be sensed even in rebuke.

Friendship – Love at its Most Disinterested

Jesus not only introduces the radical concept of servanthood into the role of leadership, he introduces the equally startling concept of friendship.

> '*My command is this; love each other as I have loved you. Greater love has no one than this that he lay down his life for his friends. You are my friends if you do what I command. I no longer call you servants, because a servant does not know his master's business. Instead I have called you friends, for every-thing that I learned from my Father I have made known to you.*'
> John 15:12–15 NIV

Not only is friendship compatible with the biblical model of leadership, it is an integral part of it. The chief characteristics to which Jesus calls attention are as follows.

Firstly, there is an equality about friendship. Friends are consciously and deliberately on the same level as far as their friendship is concerned. Perhaps that is why friendship seems often so difficult for leaders. They have to get down off their pedestal, abandon the prerogatives of their position and drop the status symbols if they are going to give and receive friend-ship. Furthermore, you don't command friends, you take them into your confidence, again something leaders often find hard to do.

Secondly there is a familiarity and an openness granted to friends; they have access to our lives so that they do not need to stand on ceremony or wait for an invitation. Nor do we have to dress up, or put on an act with them. Pretence on the one hand and flattery on the other are things that friendship cannot abide. The very disinterestedness of a friend's regard for us requires them to speak the truth at all costs. In this, friends occupy a unique position – they are close enough to be emotionally sensitive to our feelings but objective enough to be blunt when that is needed. 'Faithful are the wounds of a friend.' You can almost feel the writer wince as he pens the words.

Finally, true friendship has qualities of endurance almost beyond belief. The moral obligation of friendship is that nothing must ever be allowed to separate friends. When we understand this we realise that much of what passes today for friendship has never got past acquaintanceship. But also we can realise how much genuine friendship has to offer in cementing the bonds in a fellowship and in providing the forbearance that makes the wheels of relationships run smoothly without the need for constant problem solving.

Compassion – Love and Empathy

Compassion, or what passes for it, often suffers from being mere sentiment; we are aroused emotionally by someone's plight but we do not actually do anything about it. Robert Greenleaf warns about this when he suggests that compassion in an organisation is generally in inverse proportion to the ideals of the organisation. Then he asks this question, 'If you were really down – demoralised, humiliated, disgraced – and nothing but pure compassion, and the readiness to go the second mile in an effort to restore you as a person would help, in what kind of an institution would you stand the best chance of being restored.' His answer – 'In a business, a big business, any big business.'

Generosity – Love at its Most Liberal

The cluster of words that describe generosity could well be the pen portrait of the great leader – unselfish, open-handed, magnanimous, great spirited, large hearted, ungrudging, unstinting, chivalrous. They suggest largeness of vision, breadth of sympathies and wideness of interests.

There is an essential link between generosity and power; leaders who give themselves generously to their people and to their tasks are the ones who have power, not the leaders who husband their resources and keep things to themselves. We recognise this in the marriage relationship, those who cannot give themselves to their partners we call impotent, or powerless. Always the ungiven self is the unfulfilled self. 'One man gives freely, yet gains even more; another withholds unduly, but comes to poverty.' (Prov. 11:24)

Forgiveness – Love at its Most Gracious

No relationship will survive, let alone flourish without the willingness to forgive. Leaders need to forgive and some of them need to learn what forgiveness means – it means ceasing to blame. Leaders are in danger of keeping a scoreboard in their minds of people's failures and deficiencies, ready to be used in evidence against them if the need arises. If that is the case, there has been no forgiveness. I wonder how much leadership stress arises from this kind of unforgiveness and how many organisational problems stem from people feeling that the failures of the past are still being held against them.

Leaders also have to be ready to ask for forgiveness when they have wronged someone. With the pressure under which leaders often work and the need to make quick decisions there is always the possibility of people being treated unfairly or their legitimate rights being disregarded or overlooked. Amends need to be made quickly and honestly.

Things that Wound Love or Make Love Difficult

There are certain actions and attitudes that are particularly destructive as far as love is concerned and leaders need to be constantly aware of them, otherwise they can erode the bank of goodwill and affection that is in their favour to such an extent that when they need it most it is no longer there.

Cruelty

Physical cruelty in the church is unlikely but psychological or emotional cruelty can often be indulged in with impunity because they leave no physical bruises. The evil of cruelty is not the infliction of pain as such, because surgeons inflict pain, so do parents in disciplining their children and sports coaches pushing their charges to the limits. In all these cases however the purpose is to produce a beneficial result. With cruelty the aim is merely to make the victim suffer.

Leaders hold power and it is inevitable that they will from time to time be tempted to take advantage of that power to punish people who oppose them or to pay off old scores. We need to heed the stern judgments in scripture against unjust rulers and God's attitude to those who oppress the weak. Never think that the strong language used means that it deals with a level of injustice we would never stoop to.

Dislike

This consists of feelings of distaste or aversion or repugnance towards the other person. Leaders sometimes have to insist on people doing things that they do not want to do, or even dislike doing. It is important in these circumstances to make sure that dislike is not projected from the task on to the leader, otherwise a rift in the relationship can take place. The key lies in the attitude of the leader and the way that compliance is obtained. Always try to find out why the person dislikes the particular job or task. If it is something that is outside the range of their motivations then you need to understand the difficulty and not blame the person for their reluctance. And never insist on a person doing something that is against their conscience, even if their conscience is wrong.

Rejection

Rejection is the spurning of intimacy that has been sought or offered, and because of their position, leaders are exposed to the implications of it in several typical situations. Firstly, there

167

is a tendency for some people to feel they are rejected whenever they are corrected or reproved by the leaders. The Moravian rule needs to be taught, that everybody from time to time needs to be corrected therefore nobody should take it amiss when this occurs, nor is rebuke a valid ground to break fellowship. Secondly, there are attempts by individuals to establish levels of intimacy with leaders that are not appropriate or may even be dangerous or wrong. Such relationships should not be allowed to persist simply because the person would feel rejected. Thirdly, there is the tendency for leaders to interpret opposition to their plans or suggestions as being rejection and to take it very much to heart. Reread the section in chapter 13 on intimacy.

Ingratitude
This is taking what we can get from the other person without appreciation or thanks, sometimes without even the recognition that thanks is called for or would be appropriate. Because leaders are accustomed to their orders or requests being carried out they can very easily begin to take things and people for granted, 'That's what she is paid to do anyway.' 'That's his job.' Taking people for granted can easily become ingratitude, and ingratitude is one of our least attractive failings, lacking any graces whatsoever. It expresses the unwillingness to feel any sense of obligation towards people for what they do on our behalf.

Envy and jealousy
Because leadership sometimes appears glamorous and exciting it can readily arouse jealousy and its even more destructive cousin, envy. Leaders are also given a kind of representative status so that the success or failure of the organisation is credited to them personally. They themselves can buy into the same value system so that they see themselves or others as successes if the organisation succeeds and as failures if the organisation fails. This makes them liable to become the subjects or the objects of jealousy and envy which is ill will at the

success, popularity, privileges or achievements of others. Release from such temptations and torments is one of the blessings of becoming a servant leader and coming to realise that our responsibility is to give the job our very best and then to leave results where they belong, in the hands of God.

Neglect

Finally there is neglect which is the classic sin of omission as far as love is concerned. Neglect kills love by disappointment, by a slow process of starvation, it is care-less, indifferent, inattentive and negligent.

The inability to meet the other person's needs in a relationship is not necessarily blameworthy. What is blameworthy about neglect is that the person could have done something about it but did not care enough to make the effort.

Chapter 16

Made for Honour

We come now to what is certainly the most neglected of the four elements involved in relationships, that is, honour or respect. The Bible does not neglect it, in fact it is full of strong injunctions and commandments about the need to give honour. For example, we are to honour God (John 5:23) and our parents (Ephesians 6:2) and respect our leaders (1 Thessalonians 5:12), our employers (1 Timothy 6:1) and the King (1 Peter 2:7). Marriage as an institution is to be held in honour (Hebrews 13:4), wives are to respect their husbands (Ephesians 5:33) and husbands their wives (1 Peter 3:1,7). Widows are to be honoured (1 Timothy 5:3) so are the disadvantaged (1 Corinthians 12:23–4), in fact we are to respect everyone (1 Peter 2:17), even those who question our faith as Christians (1 Peter 3:16). What is pictured in the New Testament is, in fact a society that is built on mutual respect.

What is Honour?

When I honour or respect people, what I am doing is recognising their value or worth or dignity. But when I do so I become aware of how rich my own life is because it is surrounded and penetrated by all these valuable and worthy people. If I dishonour them, all I do is impoverish myself because I reckon my life as threadbare if it is surrounded by so much worthlessness.

Today we have a society and a mass media that seems to major on dishonour. The acid of disrespect is focused on almost everything – the past, morality, spiritual values, Christianity, marriage, parenthood and authority in any shape or form. This however, has its social costs. There is a direct correlation between the lack of respect or honour in our society and the number of people who suffer from a poor self image. The reason is not far to seek. You cannot give yourself a good self image, in spite of what all the books on pop psychology tell you. Other people create the image you get of yourself by the way they respond to you. Thus, if you are exposed to dishonour from all the sources from which you acquire your image of yourself, a negative or inadequate self image is what you will inevitably end up with.

Measures of Value

In considering worth or value as far as people are concerned, there are three measures that must be taken into account.

1. Intrinsic value.

This is, the irreducible value that every human being has because they are made in the image of God and God has given them that value. It is like the value of the gold in a gold ornament. Smash the ornament or burn it in a fire, the intrinsic value of the gold metal survives unimpaired. Some years ago our church had a long lasting relationship with a street gang in New Zealand called The Mongrel Mob. I still remember the first prayer meeting after that contact began. God spoke to us; He said, 'They are not mongrels and they are not a mob. They are young men with the potential of becoming my sons.' What God was saying was that people are never to be defined by labels, they are not the Mongrel Mob, or the Black Power, or the alcoholics, or the unemployed. They are not even the unbelievers; they are men and women and as such have eternal value that has been given or imputed by God.

2. Character.

This relates to a person's moral qualities and the standards or principles that guide their behaviour; it is what the person is rather than what they have accomplished. *'A good name is more desirable than great riches; to be esteemed is better than silver or gold.'* (Proverbs 22:1 NIV) That piece of ancient wisdom is likely to be greeted by sheer incredulity in most circles today. But in the apostolic church, character came first, it was valued above gift or ministry or charisma. If in the church today we let character go unregarded and give all the honour to talent or gift we must not be surprised if our people start building their lives round that same value system.

3. Achievement.

This is honour and respect that is due only to those who have earned it. We need to have for ourselves, and hold before our people, a commitment to excellence in everything we do. Achievement needs to be recognised, otherwise we are in danger of communicating the message that standards don't really matter all that much. For all the universality of the New Testament teaching on honour, it has no qualms about declaring that elders who direct the affairs of the church well are worthy of double honour, especially those whose work is preaching or teaching (1 Timothy 5:17).

Intrinsic value is the earliest and most important value that needs to be established in the child's life. Lack of that is one of the greatest failures of modern society. When that is established, the other measures of value can be taught and modelled and used as motivators.

But they must not be confused.

1. If intrinsic value is not established in the child, and the value of performance is emphasised, then the person feels of value only if they are achieving. Failure becomes a crippling experience, and a lack of self-worth is inevitable.

2. If the different measures of value are not distinguished, poor performance may be praised in the mistaken notion that the person's self-worth is being reinforced.

3. Criticism of poor performance can be, or can be seen to be, an attempt at character assassination, or on the other hand, poor performance is overlooked because of a person's sterling character.

Giving Meaning to Honour

Honour and respect are not words that carry any great significance or content to our modern mind, therefore we need to find alternative terms, or expressions that can restore meaning to them or help us to recover their original sense. Otherwise I may say 'I respect you' but the words can have as much meaning as if I said, 'I think you are 1.8m tall.' Here are some terms that help to illuminate what is meant by honour or respect.

1. Acceptance.
Notice that by acceptance we do not mean mere tolerance or the passive accommodation to something that is inevitable. Acceptance is an active receiving of the person in a way that says, 'You are a valuable addition to this team, or this department or this company.' That kind of acknowledgment from leaders is very important in making people feel they are recognised as worthy participants in the activity.

2. Affirmation.
This seeks to enhance people's sense of self worth and self confidence by drawing attention to their strengths and abilities. The message it communicates is, 'I think you are marvellous and I would like you to feel that way about yourself.' The pay-off as far as leaders are concerned is enormous; there are few things more exhilarating than leading a team of people who feel good about themselves because they have strengths and know what they are. Sadly, much of our teaching in the church seems aimed at making people feel badly about themselves.

3. Appreciation.
This is more subjective, it expresses my pleasure or satisfaction or gratification with who you are or with what you are doing. It

says in effect, 'I enjoy seeing you the way you are and doing the things you do.' Genuine appreciation expressed by leaders is one of the rewards that count for most with people.

4. Admiration.
Admiration draws attention to the person's achievements and with it, expresses the desire to emulate them. It says, 'You set a standard in this that impresses me, and one that would make me proud if I could attain it too.'

Admiration is an even more powerful stimulus than appreciation, particularly when it is forthcoming from leaders who presumably are people who know what they are talking about. Appreciation says 'Well done!' but there is the assumption, 'I could have done it as well as that too.' Admiration says frankly, 'I could never have done it as well as that!'

5. Acknowledgment.
This is giving the person recognition and praise publicly or in the presence of other people. But leaders should be careful not just to speak well of their people to third parties, but also to say it to people's faces. If they get to hear about the former, they may be gratified, but if they never hear the latter they are also likely to think 'Why don't they say it to me too?'

How Do You Show Honour or Respect?

The issue of respect is a crucial one for the quality of the relationship between leaders and people. People who are in a subordinate role can easily begin to feel that they are taken for granted, or that no regard is paid to their feelings or their rights, and that they are being 'treated like dirt.' I suspect that many industrial disputes, ostensibly over pay, stem from such feelings amongst workers who have decided that if they are going to treat us like machines or worse, they are going to have to pay for it.

People give of their best only when they feel respected. The person who is honoured and knows it, has a great stake in behaving honourably. The one who is persistently dishon-oured, eventually sees no point in doing anything otherthan living down to people's expectations. Here are some of the main ways in which leaders can honour their people or show respect for them.

1. Saying so, that is, expressing it in words, spoken or writ-ten, in the form of thanks, commendation, approval, praise or appreciation for work well done or services rendered.

2. Acknowledging people's presence in company or sup-porting them in public. Just as people honour their leaders by this kind of identification and acknowledgment, 'our' minister, 'our' elders', so leaders honour their people by similar acknow-ledgements. 'My house church leaders, and I'm proud of them and the job they are doing', or 'one of the people I can always rely on to give their best.' (2 Peter 3:15–16)

3. Taking them into your confidence. For example;

(a) Seeking their opinion or advice on matters affecting the organisation, and treating their views seriously.
(b) Submitting proposed policies or courses of action for their critique and input, and taking their criticisms seriously.
(c) Explaining fully the reasons behind decisions you have made that affect them directly or indirectly, and
(d) Sharing bad news with them as well as good news.

4. Acknowledging their right in their private lives to:

(a) Make decisions you would not make,
(b) Make mistakes you would not make,
(c) Hold views you do not hold, and
(d) Follow the dictates of their own conscience.

5. Treating people as responsible adults and refusing to let them get away with shoddy work, or with a level of performance that is below what we know they can achieve. If we let them get away with inferior performance we are saying in effect, 'That is all I believe you are capable of.'

6. Honour is also however conveyed non-verbally. Regard or respect is communicated not merely by what we say, but by

the tone of voice, the look in our eyes and our bearing towards one another. Our eyes and tone of voice are dead give-aways because we cannot control them with our will. If I feel unfriendly towards you I may be able to say friendly words but a friendly warmth in my voice and a friendly glance in my eye I cannot fake.

7. Honour is also conveyed by what I call 'being present' for the other, in other words we are consciously present and attentive to them when we are in communication with one another. If you go into your superior's office to talk to him about something you think is important, how do you feel if all the time you are speaking he is fumbling in his desk drawer or jotting down a memo for his secretary? Ignored – dishonoured. But if he shoves his papers aside, says to his secretary, 'No calls for 20 minutes' and then says to you 'Sit down, I want to hear this', how do you feel then? You respond, as we all do, to being honoured.

What Damages Respect

There are few things more shattering for leaders who have been accustomed to being looked up to and treated with deference, than to find their people no longer respect them. Respect is not however, invulnerable, and it can gradually crumble or erode without leaders being aware of what is happening. Respect, once lost, is also very difficult to win back and it always takes time to do so.

Here are some of the things in the leaders' character or performance that can lose them the respect of their people.

1. Inadequacy, incompetence or repeated failures.
Not every failure, or even a string of failures is necessarily disastrous as far as respect for leaders is concerned. The following however, are generally fatal:

(a)   Failures in the essential leadership functions.
      I may respect the leaders' preaching gifts, counselling skills and personal characters', but if they are totally

inadequate and inept as leaders then I cannot respect them as a leadership I can safely follow.

(b) Failure in areas in which the person has claimed to be competent.

No one is likely to lose respect for me because I am no good at strategic planning, unless I get a job in charge of corporate planning. Then I am likely to lose the respect of my stafff very quickly.

(c) Failure that occurs because the leader did not really try.

We are unlikely to lose people's respect if we give the job our best shot and still fail, but we will lose it soon if it is realised that we made only half hearted efforts.

2. Irresponsibility or selfishness.

People lose respect very quickly for leaders who are self seeking or irresponsible. It is interesting that no human society, past or present has been found in which the selfish man is admired. Some have admired the cruel man, or the vengeful man, or the treacherous man but nobody has ever admired the selfish man.

3. Self pity or self indulgence.

Leaders who grumble about their difficult lot or are seen to be hard on other people but soft on themselves soon lose people's respect. Leaders are expected to be better than most at handling difficult times without giving up or giving in.

4. The inability to stand up under pressure.

The moral weakness of leaders who abandon their stated principles because of opposition or influence from outside or within the organisation soon loses them respect from their people, even although the outcome may turn out to be easier or more favourable than before. People find it hard to respect leaders who lack the courage of their convictions.

5. All forms of domination or manipulation.

Leaders who use people for their own ends rapidly forgo their respect. There is an implicit understanding that leadership is a position of trust and it is misused if it is perverted to serve the ends of the leaders.

There are also a number of common attitudes and behaviour patterns that leaders sometimes adopt towards the people under them that are essentially dishonouring or show a lack of respect for the people. They should be understood and studiously avoided.

1. Disparagement, nagging and fault finding.
There is a world of difference between the necessary assessment of performance or the pointing out of failure with a view to its amendment and the censorious criticism that attacks the worth of the person and damages his self respect. Leaders must always make a clear distinction in their minds between who a person is and what a person does. Proper discipline begins by being able to say, 'I want you on the team and you are totally acceptable here'. Only then can it go on to say 'Neither of us can be satisfied with this level of performance. Let's see what can be done about it.'

2. Embarrassing people by putting them down in public or drawing public attention to their weaknesses or failure.
Sometimes humour can be barbed, and used to pillory a person who has failed. Such a person is in a very vulnerable position and it is easy to score points off them. Making a public spectacle of them, even in joke form will certainly do nothing to improve their performance or your standing with their colleagues. But protect their feelings and you earn their undying goodwill.

3. Ignoring or disregarding people's rights and all forms of exploitation or discrimination are deeply dishonouring towards the people concerned and spring from a lack of understanding of the dignity and value of the human person.

Chapter 17

Understanding Understanding

It is an axiom that if you are ever going to lead people successfully you must both know them and understand them. What is more the people you lead must also know you and understand you. Jesus repeatedly emphasised this essential relationship between leaders and led, and he modelled it in his own leadership.

> *'I am the good shepherd; I know my sheep and my sheep know me.'*   John 10:14 NIV

> *'To him the gatekeeper opens; the sheep hear his voice, and he calls his own sheep by name and leads them out.'*
>   John 10:3 RSV

This is much more than merely knowing who are the sheep, it means knowing who the sheep are, in other words it means knowing them. A name in the Bible always signifies much more than simply a title or a means of identification, it stands for the character or the cluster of consistent traits that make up a particular personality. Thus the shepherd knows, not just the names the sheep recognise when they are called, but he understands them, their characters, their temperaments, and their individual idiosyncracies.

Obviously as the organisation gets larger the leaders at the top will not be able to know personally more than a small percentage of the people involved. The principle nevertheless remains the same, they must know and understand the individuals in the next level below them, that they are personally directing and who are personally responsible to them. Those leaders in turn must know their subordinates and so on down the chain to the first level supervisors.

The Desire for Understanding

The longing to be understood is one of the primary needs that draws us towards relationships. We crave to really know some other person and in turn to be known by them. *'Then I shall know fully, even as I am fully known'* (1 Corinthians 13:12 NIV)

But at the same time we intuitively recognise the vulnerability of being known like that, because if I am really known and understood, I stand naked before the other person, with all the possibilities of hurt and rejection. From that exposure we flee like Adam in the Garden, *'I was afraid because I was naked, so I hid'* (Genesis 3:10 NIV).

That is why we so often avoid the risk and settle for projecting images of ourselves that we hope may gain us acceptance with this group or that. These image are expendable, if one is rejected, it doesn't matter to us all that much because we are not really 'in' it. We can simply abandon it and try another variant that offers a better chance of success.

Images have become one of the accepted trappings of leadership today. To capture the heart of the people, we are told, you have to project the right kind of image. PR consultants, advertising agencies, speech writers and political managers are all in the image making business. The reasoning apparently is that even if you cannot fool all the people all the time, if you are going to succeed you have to try and fool as many of the people for as much of the time as you can. That may seem unkind, but if the image is not the truth about the person it is essentially counterfeit and deceptive. One of the reasons for the widespread mistrust of leaders at every level of society is because of the awareness of the hollowness of the images that are used to entice our support and capture our loyalty. Sadly, a preoccupation with images has also become part of the repertoire of too many Christian leaders.

The Beginning and the End

The desire for understanding is not only the end or goal of relationships, it is also the prerequisite for the other elements of a relationship to survive.

> I cannot care for somebody I do not know, because I may totally misunderstand what their needs are.
> I cannot trust somebody I do not know, because that trust may prove to be sheer and reckless presumption, and
> I cannot truly honour somebody I do not know, because it would be like giving value to an unknown quantity.

This is important so that we appreciate that knowing and understanding people is not just an optional extra, to be recommended if you are really interested, but one that can be done without if the effort proves too burdensome.

How Do You Know a Person?

The knowledge of persons is by no means self evident or we would not have the problems we experience with understanding each other. Partly our difficulty is that our motivation to understand is not on a par with our craving to be understood. And partly it is because we realise that knowing a person in any real way is going to be a long term assignment. The human psyche has tremendous depths and complexities and to know a person in depth sometimes takes a lifetime. Our modern impatient society leaves us very ill equipped for such long term voyages of discovery so that most people settle for very superficial relationships and wonder why they are dying of loneliness inside.

Obviously a leader cannot know all his people to the same

level of deep intimacy, but know and understand them to some degree he must. Here are some of the key issues involved.

1. Firstly, to 'know' a person takes place essentially at the level of spirit therefore it is largely an intuitive apprehension. You can observe a person's behaviour patterns, note their opinions about a whole range of subjects and see how they react to various situations or circumstances but all that is merely information about the person. Knowing the essential being of a person, that is, who the person is in themselves, is a quite different matter, it is discerned or perceived with our spirit. That is why you can work alongside the same person for ten or fifteen years but at the end of that time realise you do not really know them at all. On the other hand you can meet another person for the first time and almost immediately have a clear and convincing sense of the kind of person you are dealing with.

2. Secondly however, knowledge of persons is also dependent on self disclosure. That means that we will 'know' a person only if, and only to the extent that they reveal themselves. Some people are, as we say, 'an open book', they are transparently obvious in everything they do. Other people are closed, enigmatic, secretive, so that you can only guess at what is going on in their minds.

Self disclosure cannot be forced upon people, nor can they be tricked into it. What leaders have to do therefore is create an atmosphere of mutual trust and acceptance within which people will feel safe enough to voice their real opinions, share their real feelings and let their real self be known. But that requires that there be a similar openness and self disclosure on the part of the leaders. They also have to be willing to be known. Often however, the least open people in a church tend to be the leaders; they want and encourage openness on the part of their people but they do not want to take the risk of themselves being open to the people for fear of losing their confidence or support.

Consider the implications of the following propositions for leaders who genuinely desire to serve their people.

1. You cannot serve people effectively unless you know them,
2. You will not know people unless they are open to you,
3. They will not be open to you unless they trust you,
4. They will not trust you unless they know you,
5. They will not know you unless you are open to them.

The openness we are talking about is not necessarily or even primarily a matter of telling people a lot about ourselves. That can amount to image-making in any case. It is an inner attitude of honesty and transparency that is willing to be seen for what we are and is prepared to take the same risks in openness of heart and spirit as we expect other people to take towards us. What clouds that openness is more often a protectiveness towards disclosing weaknesses or failures or the fear of honest communication of our thoughts and feelings. The result of these attitudes is the erection of barriers between us and other people that give them the impression they are always being held at a distance.

What Should Leaders Know About Their People?

Regardless of the goals and objectives that may represent the task of an organisation, a primary responsibility of Christian leaders is the empowering of their people, or as Paul expresses it, *'to prepare God's people for works of service'* (Ephesians 4:12 NIV) This means,

1. Discovering what God's purpose and design is for them as individuals,
2. Stewarding them so that they reach fulfilment by coming as close to God's design for them as possible, and
3. Dealing with the hindrances and barriers that stand in the way of them reaching this correspondence with God's design.

Discovering and Describing Giftedness

This section is based on experience with a process known as S.I.M.A. (System for Identifying Motivated Abilities) developed by Arthur Miller and Ralph Mattson and is used with permission of the proprietors People Management Inc., 10 Station Road, Simsbury, Connecticut).

The biblical view of man establishes six key factors that are critical for understanding the nature of individual giftedness.

1. Every individual is unique. God is the Creator and the mark of creativity is always originality therefore each human being in the mix of his or her God-given strengths and interests is unique and inimitable. Individuals are therefore not to be put into boxes, classed into categories, compared with anyone else or measured against statistical averages.

2. The mark of God's gifts in a person's life is that they work. Nothing effective is ever accomplished anywhere by anybody without using God's gifts. Even unbelieving man cannot build a house, run a business, paint a portrait, cook a stew or play a game of golf or do anything effectively without having to use God's gifts. That is why the Bible says He makes even the wrath of man to praise Him.

3. Man is made to God's design and design is the ability to plan and develop with a particular purpose or intention in view. Because we were each created to fulfil a purpose we have been equipped by God with the capacity to be good at some things but not good at everything, to excel at some tasks but not at every task. Successful people are always those who know or have discovered what their strengths are, and spend the rest of their life getting better and better at what they are already good at doing.

4. Not only are God's gifts in a person's life the means for them to perform effectively, they are also the source of their satisfaction and enjoyment. When they are engaged in purposeful activity, in other words when they are using God's gifts, they not only produce good work they actually enjoy themselves in the process. When using these gifts and abilities they never get bored, never get under pressure and never need to be driven to use them. In these areas they are self starters and self motivated. God, it seems, has created us in such a way that when we are pouring ourselves out to serve him through the

very capacities he himself has given us to do it with, there is joy built into it for us.

5. A person's strengths and interests are gifts, that is, they do not earn or create them, they are given, therefore the person is accountable to the Giver for their use. God expects us to accept responsibility for stewarding or wisely managing and capitalising on the abilities he has entrusted to us.

6. Because the deposit of God given gifts is innate, that is, they are there from birth, a person's motivations and strengths are consistent throughout their whole life span. They will use the abilities with greater degrees of competency and complexity as they mature but the pattern of strengths remains consistent throughout the whole life-span. It follows that if we discover a person's pattern of abilities, we have something that is highly predictive. If in the past they functioned most effectively and most harmoniously within a certain range of abilities we know that they will always function best when they are using those same capacities. The motivated abilities pattern therefore becomes the key to the most effective use of human resources, both in terms of productivity and in terms of fulfilment. Both go together; we are most productive when we are most fulfilled in what we do. We are least productive when what we do is frustrating or unsatisfying.

Misuse of Human Resources

In spite of man's advanced technologies and his increasing knowledge of human nature, studies on the mismatch between the abilities and strengths of employees and job requirements paint a sad picture.

Management researcher Daniel Yankelovich reports that only 13 percent of the U.S. workforce find their work truly meaningful and a survey of 350,000 employees from 7,000 corporations showed that only 20 percent considered they were in jobs that made good use of their talents.

Business and industry still labour, it seems, under a work philosophy based on the mechanistic model of human nature that says that the worker can be adapted to the job or trained to fulfill the requirements of the job provided only that the inducements are right. The result is the enormous amount of stress, boredom, mediocre performance and dissatisfaction that is to be found in our modern industrialised societies.

It is not only employers who are to blame. People persistently make blunders in choosing careers or vocations that are unsuitable to them or make mistakes in the course of their careers as follows:

1. Trying to develop skills and strengths that they have never been given in the first place.
2. Paying too much attention to trying to correct what they see as weaknesses and incapacities instead of concentrating on excelling in the areas in which they are strong.
3. Choosing goals without understanding their motivations so they end up pursuing a goal that is right for somebody else, but wrong for them. The result is that they either run out of motivation and fail to achieve the goal or they stick at it until they have achieved it but then find it unfulfilling and unsatisfying.

Contents of a Motivated Abilities Pattern

Miller and Mattson have developed a Motivated Abilities Pattern that identifies for each person, five basic factors and a number of different elements making up each factor. The factors with just a few of the hundreds of possible elements are as follows:

1. Motivated abilities.

Among all the abilities a person possesses there is a cluster of about 6 to 10 that they are positively motivated to use. A person will always do their most effective work using these abilities. Examples are planning, organising, investigating, developing, teaching, overseeing, communicating. In each category there are specific ways of functioning, for example some people plan by setting goals, others by strategising and others by making detailed lists of things that have to be done. Some people develop by maximising results, others by adapting or modifying or by building relationships.

2. Subject matter.

These are things that a person is motivated to work with or work through. They may range from very tangible, concrete things like machinery or constructions to highly abstract concepts, ideas or principles. They may include logistics, people, systems, information and data, policies, techniques or visual elements. Usually a person has 5 to 7 types of subject matter that are positively motivating for them.

3. Circumstances.

There are certain situational elements or circumstances that trigger a person's motivation or keep him interested or enhance her productivity. For example, some people need clear goals and instructions at the outset of an assignment, others plan as they go, some people thrive under pressure or in situations they have never faced before, others need time to prepare for new challenges, some look for response as a form of feedback or for measurable results, others insist on precision or quality in everything they do. Usually there are 5 to 7 elements that identify what amount of structure we need, what results we look for, what arouses our interest or keeps us interested and what type of work environment suits us best.

4. Operating relationships.

Every person is motivated to maintain a particular type of relationship with other people in a work or group situation. For example one person is an individualist, another wants to be a member of a team, one wants to lead or manage other people, another acts as a co-ordinator or a mediator in disputes, one person is a kind of spark plug always sparking off new ideas and another is a facilitator or a trainer of others or functions best in a supportive role.

In the same way different people flourish best under different management styles. One person needs a hands-off manager who sets goals and objectives but allows people to set their own priorities and take responsibility for the way the job is done. Another needs a supportive manager prepared to assist or intervene at critical stages in the operation and another looks for a collaborative style of management where their input into the policy and decisionmaking process is received and welcomed.

5. The central motivational thrust.
This is both the motor that drives a person's motivation and also the one particular result or outcome that the person is motivated to seek in everything they do. For some it is drive to excel or be the best, or to face challenges or tests and put their abilities always on the line, to another it is to impact and shape people or things or situations, or to gain demonstrable competence in a number of areas, or to gain a response from people and influence their behaviour. Some people get their stimulus from the process they are involved in, to others the completion of the task or the accomplishment of the goal is all important. A person has one main thrust and sometimes a secondary or subsidiary one in addition.

Understanding How People Work

The Motivated Abilities Pattern is a unique tool that enables the best use to be made of a person's strengths and interests, it identifies problems caused by job mismatch, enables teams to be built with the specific capacities and abilities needed for a project or assignment, and illuminates how different people respond differently in a team leadership or eldership. It is also of inestimable value in making the hard decisions as to which of a number of people being considered for a job that none of them have done before, have the capacities to succeed in the new role. Thus it can be used very effectively in identifying leadership potential because the specific capacities needed can be detected in the way a person has functioned in the achievements he has found most satisfying and enjoyable.

Things That Hinder Understanding

Here are some of the things that hinder understanding or cause misunderstandings to arise between people. We could divide them broadly into problems associated with the information or the message we send or give out to people, and problems with our perception of the information or messages we receive from people.

Problems with message sending

1. Lack of communication or inadequate communication.

Today there is a ready market for books and seminars on communication, creative listening, body language and so on, and they can be helpful. But they can also be bought to learn techniques that will give us the edge in the communication contest. In such cases they are non productive and even counter productive. Real understanding of persons comes out of a deep respect for the integrity of the other person and the willingness to take the same risks of openness and self disclosure that they are called to take.

2. Lack of self knowledge or self awareness.

A person who does not really know themselves cannot share themselves. This is often the problem with children who are asked by frustrated parents, 'Why do you do things like that?' and answer 'I don't know'. At a certain age that is the truth.

3. Personality traits.

Shyness, or reserve, and feelings of inferiority or inadequacy make communication difficult even about simple things because the person feels that nothing they could share is important enough to interest anybody.

4. Having an image of the other person as aloof or rejecting.

This is often the case with the image people have of leaders, and sometimes it is the image leaders deliberately create.

5. Differing perceptions.
Difficulties arise sometimes because of the differing perceptions as to the degree of intimacy or closeness appropriate to
the relationship, or sometimes because of the natural swing
between the desire for intimacy and the desire for privacy.

6. Lack of time or opportunity to communicate.
Real communication in a way that is self revealing cannot be
turned on at a moments notice, or operate tidily at set times.
Thus time, particularly informal time, must be allowed for real
understanding to develop between leaders and people.
Whether this happens or not depends largely on the level of
importance that leadership places on understanding and good
communication. It is not time wasted, though the task oriented
leader finds that hard to take seriously.

7. Emotional hurt or woundedness.
When this has taken place, particularly in childhood, it has
created in the person an extreme vulnerability to the prospect
of being rejected. Therefore it seems safer not to risk close
contact at all.

8. Difference between the parties.
Sometimes differences in age, education, status, sex, and personality inhibit communication and therefore understanding.

Problems with perception

Sometimes the problem is at the receiving end, that is we
misunderstand or misinterpret the information or messages
that are being sent to us by the other person. Some of the
common causes of this are –

1. Bias, prejudice or dogmatism.
These are generally fixed stereotypes or presuppositions, that
are generally unexamined, and often unconscious. They condition our perceptions as to what is being said or communicated.

2. Insensitivity or lack of imagination.
This is an inability to enter the other person's frame of reference, particularly if it is different from our own, so as to be able to really understand what they are saying or communicating.

3. Hasty judgments.
Sometimes a person will jump to conclusions on the basis of only a small part of the message. Before the message is completed or all the information received, they already 'know' what is meant.

4. Language, cultural or personality differences.

5. The inability or the unwillingness to listen properly.
Often we are not really listening at all, we are busily thinking of what we are going to say as soon as the other person runs out of breath.

6. Different associations or the differing emotive content of the same words to different people.
Words often have an emotional loading affected by our past experiences. Generally the thing we are least aware of is the emotive content of our communication.

7. Lack of empathy or mistaken interpretation of the other person's feelings.
When we decide we know how the other person is feeling we can begin to interpret the actual words in terms of those feelings. For example if we mistakenly decide the person is angry or upset we can take a perfectly genuine expression of praise or approval as being sarcasm.

Chapter 18

Meet the Corporation

So far we have considered a number of the elements of the leader's environment – goals, plans, time, people, facilities, logistics, systems and so on. But there is something else that may be more important than all of these put together and yet is probably least understood of all.

Can you recall the first time you joined a company or took over the leadership of a church and very soon became aware of being, as it were, in a different culture. There were certain different ways of doing things from those you were familiar with, the people related to each other in distinctive ways, they shared certain common attitudes, and sometimes even ways of speaking about others, or behaving towards people outside the organisation.

Moreover, loyalty and commitment and service were apparently demanded or expected towards something called 'the company' or 'the church'. It wasn't to the managers or leaders as such because they were themselves committed to and serving the same ends as hard as anybody, or harder. And yet, when you looked at them, the people, as people, were not observably much different as individuals from the people in other organisations or other churches.

After a while the strangeness wears off and we become habituated to the life and culture of the organisation so that its ways become user friendly. We have the odd feeling however, of having become 'its' lackey, and having to please 'it' to get on, but we don't really know what 'it' is. To understand the issues involved here we have to trace its origins and development in the one place where its inner history has been written, that is, in Scripture.

The Creation Mandate

In Genesis 1:27–28 NIV we have what is generally called the Creation Mandate, sometimes the Dominion Mandate, sometimes the Cultural Mandate. It is the authority that God gave humankind over the world that he had made, to unfold its potential and to steward its resources.

> *'So God created man in his own image, in the image of God he created him; male and female he created them. God blessed them and said to them, Be fruitful and increase in number; fill the earth and subdue it. Rule over the fish of the sea and the birds of the air, and over every living creature that moves on the ground.'*

The creation mandate has two components:

1. Be fruitful and increase in number.
This began to be fulfilled with the beginning of the first human family in Genesis 4:1–2.

2. Rule over the earth and everything in it.
This began to be fulfilled with the building of the first city in Genesis 4:17:

> *'Cain was then building a city, and he named it after his son Enoch.'*

Henceforth much of Bible history, indeed much of all human history is the history of the city – Sodom and Gomorrah, Babylon and Nineveh, Tyre and Sidon, Rome, Damascus,

Jerusalem, Athens – the city is everywhere. It becomes the centre of civilisation and culture, the hub of commerce, trade and wealth, the birthplace of political power and the mainspring of military conquest. It is significant that the first nations were coalitions of city states and the first empires were founded on cities. But the city also spawns oppression, injustice and slavery and becomes the fountainhead of idolatry, the occult and the magic arts.

The city, in fact, becomes the enduring Old Testament embodiment for the reality that Paul and the other New Testament writers have in mind when they speak about powers, rulers, thrones, dominions, authorities and principalities. Consider the following important aspects of the development of this theme.

1. The city stands as the symbol for all of man's corporate endeavours, whatever the scale of them. Thus, at the macro level the city stands for the nation or the culture, or the society as a whole. Thus the judgments against the nations are generally judgments against cities. But at the micro level the city represents the individual business or institution or organisation or club or church or family. Each is a 'city'.

2. The city is named, and when the city is named it gains an identity and a character of its own. Thus Nineveh is 'the bloody city' (Nahum 3:1) Babylon is 'the mother of harlots' (Revelation 17:5) Tyre is 'the jubilant city' (Isaiah 23:7) and Jerusalem is Ariel, 'the lion of God' (Isaiah 29:1).

3. The city becomes a 'power'. This is a very important concept to grasp. It means that when a city is established by the corporate decisions and actions of a group of men and women, there very early comes into being a corporate spirit or persona that becomes a created reality in its own right.

While to begin with it is plastic and can be shaped or formed, as time goes on the corporate spirit becomes increasingly independent of the people who created it in the first place. It acquires a character and a life of its own, instead of being shaped by people, it shapes people to its own design. Set up originally to serve the ends of its makers, the power that is the city now uses people for its own ends. It often outlasts its founders and may even turn against them and expel them if they become superfluous or a hindrance to goals it has in view.

The city's predominant instinct is for continuance, therefore it will do anything to survive. Thus Babylon declares:

> 'I will continue forever – the eternal queen...
> I will never be a widow or suffer the loss of children'

I remember some years ago seeing a television interview of the then Prime Minister of New Zealand in which he was asked 'Mr Prime Minister, what is the first principle of government?' You might expect the answer to have been, 'The first principle of government is to govern.' Oh no. The Prime Minister got it dead right. 'The first principle of government' he said, 'is to stay in power'.

4. Because of the Fall, the city, man's creation, is also fallen, therefore it becomes the expression of mankind's corporate rebellion against God; 'come let us build for ourselves a city' (Genesis 11:4) – Babel. Because of its rebellion the city becomes idolatrous, that is, it always seeks to become the ultimate authority and the ultimate dispenser of power. What was in embryo in Babel has become full blown.

God says,

> *'so that from the rising of the sun to the place of its setting men may know there is none besides me. I am the Lord, and there is no other.'* Isaiah 45:5, 6 NIV

Babylon says,

> *'I am and there is none besides me.'* Isaiah 47:8, 10 NIV

Nineveh, the carefree city,

> *'said to herself "I am and there is none besides me"'*
> Zephaniah 2:15 NIV

Tyre, in the pride of her heart says,

> '*I am a god; I sit on the throne of a god in the heart of the seas*'
> Ezekiel 28:2 NIV.

This idolatrous drive for ultimacy is by no means restricted to the ancient cities of antiquity, it is rampant in corporation boardrooms, state bureaucracies, football teams and sometimes church and denominational institutions. I remember reading an article some years ago in a business review where the statement was made that in considering applicants for top executive posts in large corporations, to have a happy marriage was a mark against your suitability. The reasoning was that a man with a happy marriage would not give his ultimate loyalty and commitment solely to his job. That seems to me to be the appalling cynicism of the city.

5. There is a further issue that is even more serious and has to be reckoned with. Firstly, in the Fall man lost his spiritual authority over the world, and secondly, into the power vacuum thus created, the devil came. Satan the ruler of the demons becomes the ruler of the world system; he becomes '*the god of the present age*'. (2 Corinthians 4:4, 1 John 5:19, Matthew 4:8–10, John 12:31). This position Satan uses to establish his demonic 'powers' in the spiritual realm dominating the fallen structural powers.

> '*For our struggle is not against flesh and blood but against the rulers, against the authorities, against the powers of this dark world and against the spiritual forces of evil in the heavenly realms*'
> Ephesians 6:12 NIV

Jacques Ellul points out that the Hebrew word for city also means 'The Watching Angel', therefore behind the structural power, the corporate spirit that is the city, there stands the watching angel, the demonic power in the heavenly realm that is the idol or the god that is worshipped in the city. The Bible names many of these demonic powers – Baal, Ashtoreth, Molech, Dagon, Chemosh, Diana, Marduck and others.

6. In considering the devastating effects of the Fall therefore, we must take serious account of rebellion against the will of God and thus evil, from three sources:

(a)   The personal rebellion and sin of fallen men and women.
(b)   The corporate rebellion of fallen structures, the inner spirit or persona of organisations, cultures and societies, and therefore structural evil in society.
(c)   Demonic evil and opposition from Satan and his powers and authorities in the spirit realm.

These three areas need to be clearly identified because the factors involved and the way to deal with them are different in each case.

How the City Operates

The discussion so far may help to clarify what is behind some of the more frustrating dynamics that leaders in organisations have to face. Consider, for example, the following –

1. The sometimes rigid, implacable, or irrational resistance to change on the part of otherwise mellow, adaptable and progressive men and women. You are not up against people as individuals, you are opposed by the 'power', the corporate spirit of the institution whether it is a denominational structure or a business corporation or a school board. The 'power' will use people to frustrate your plans if it can, and you will notice that it is rarely very particular about the methods it uses to do so.

2. Why in a big organisation there is often the person who is a typical 'gold-bricker.' He skimps his work, slides out of the difficult jobs and passes the buck when something goes wrong. But when the promotions come out, lo and behold he seems always to get on. We may say he toadies to the boss, or drinks with the right crowd but it is neither; he is someone who has yielded to the corporate spirit of the organisation. If you do, you can break all the rules but the power will still look after you.

On the other hand there is the employee who is conscientious, diligent and dedicated in everything she does but somehow when the plum jobs come up she always misses out to someone much less able or reliable. In the top echelons there is a feeling that she somehow doesn't 'fit'. It has nothing to do with her personality or her work but with a sense that she doesn't really 'belong' here. What you have here is someone who consciously or unconsciously refuses to yield to the corporate spirit of the place. The point is that if you don't yield spiritual allegiance to the power, it will try to destroy you or get rid of you, even although you do everything right and keep all the rules.

3. The power struggle that takes place at an impalpable level in a business takeover. Here you have one 'city' trying to swallow another and the other fighting for survival. It also explains why, after the takeover, certain of the management team from the absorbed organisation are rapidly and ruthlessly dumped and replaced, almost regardless of their capabilities. They are ones who have grievously offended the conquering 'power'.

4. Why a church split is so painful and catastrophic and often leaves the people involved deeply scarred and wounded. The corporate spirit, called by John in Revelation the 'angel' of the church has been amputated and is sometimes left permanently handicapped. At the same time any new church that may be established out of the split begins with a wounded 'angel' created out of the resentment or hurt of the individuals who are its founders.

Even a church that deliberately divides as a means of growth suffers at the same level of corporate spirit. No matter how harmonious and desired the division is, you can count on a time of corporate bereavement in the church that remains while it works through the sense of loss and separation.

5. Why at a football match the team's army of supporters are somehow swamped by a group mind, so that they are totally one-eyed about the game, by group emotions, so that a goal for our team produces near euphoria and by group behaviour, including singing, flag waving, cheering and so on. A football game is actually a good place to observe the corporate spirit in raw action, sometimes including the demonic element when mindless violence can erupt for no apparent reason.

6. The presence of a demonic power operating behind the structural power is not only, or even primarily manifested in blatant violence. It can as readily function in the corporate boardroom or the council chambers where the emotional level never rises above that of civilised conversation. Nevertheless a suprahuman dimension of evil can be at work, manifested sometimes in the bland amorality of the decisions reached, or in the confusion and obfuscation of ethical issues and at other times with the sense of something or someone vastly and malevolently wise that is manipulating the strings and operating the puppets.

It is the pervasiveness and seemingly omnipotent nature of these powers in our culture and society that creates the feeling of helplessness amongst most Christians towards the secular world and keeps them content to stay within the safe houses of their churches. In the church meetings they can sing the triumphant songs of Zion and feel conquerors and victorious and reigning with Jesus in heavenly places. But in the world they feel utterly impotent against the power of the institutions that pervade their lives. These powers demand their allegiance, by their services maintain their secure way of life, and control their future and their happiness. I wonder to what extent some of the end time scenarios of popular eschatology are in fact the rationalising of this position so that we can live with a weak response to evil in society without feeling failures.

Christ and the Powers

We have examined elsewhere the significance of the life, death and resurrection of Jesus in terms of power. In the present context it bears repetition because it is insufficiently understood and yet it lies at the very heart of our ability to live and work in the power structures of the world without being dominated by them and, more importantly to establish the lordship of Christ over the powers themselves.

199

> *'His intent was that now, through the church, the manifold wisdom of God should be made known to the rulers and authorities in the heavenly realms.'*   Ephesians 3:10 NIV

Firstly we see that in the Incarnation Jesus invaded the realms of the 'powers'. He came into a country that was specifically dominated by the powers, in at least four dimensions.

1.   A strong and cruel military power, the Roman Empire. Palestine was an occupied country; there were foreign troops stationed there.
2.   A harsh, legalistic and repressive religious power, the synagogue and the Sanhedrin, that tried to assassinate Jesus just because he healed on the Sabbath day.
3.   The economic power of the Herodians that farmed out the tax collection and bled the country white.
4.   The Satanic power presiding over the fallen structural powers. There are some grounds for believing that there may have been a mass eruption of demonic activity and a severe infestation of much of the population in the period preceding the coming of Christ.

Secondly, Jesus lived in the midst of the powers but he lived a life that was absolutely free of their dominance. Moreover he deliberately demonstrated that freedom. This explains for example why he repeatedly healed the sick and cast out demons on the sabbath day and in the synagogues. He was refusing to yield to the spirit of the synagogue. It is behind his reply to the threat of Herod to kill him, *'Go and tell that fox, "Behold I cast out demons and perform cures today and tomorrow, and the third day I finish my course."'* (Luke 13:32 RSV) and his response to Pilate, *'You would have no power over me, unless it had been given you from above'* (John 19:11 RSV).

But when he came to the end of his ministry, Jesus suddenly surrenders to the powers. He surrenders to the religious power, the Sanhedrin; it hands him over to the military power, the Roman Procurator who ordered his crucifixion while the economic power stripped him stark naked and gambled his clothes away. Strangest of all Jesus surrendered to the Satanic power. He said *'This is your hour and the power of darkness.'* (Luke 22:53 RSV)

But here is the truth that needs to be repeatedly pondered and reflected on until we grasp its significance.

Jesus' death was the ultimate act of obedience to the Father's will. *'Not my will, but yours be done'.* That act of obedience, to death, even death on the Cross, just because it was the Father's will, exhausted, debilitated and neutralised the rebellion of the powers.

Rebellion is what energises the 'powers' large or small, the drive to be the ultimate authority over men and women, to be the reason for their service and the object of their worship, the drive that says 'I am and there is no one besides me'. But the utter obedience of Jesus to the will of God was something that the powers could not handle; they could not stir him into rebellion. Neither injustice or abuse or challenge to his integrity, or mockery, or the instinct for self preservation or the sight of his mother, or death or hell itself could deviate him one hairsbreadth from obedience to the Father's will.

The powers could do no more, the devil, the primal fount of all rebellion against God, could do no more. They were defeated, disarmed, rendered impotent before that Man.

Then death itself succumbed – he rose again!

> *'And having disarmed the powers and authorities, he made a public spectacle of them, triumphing over them by the cross.'*
> Colossians 2:15 NIV

> *'…He raised him from the dead and seated him at his right hand in the heavenly realms, far above all rule and authority, power and dominion and every title that can be given, not only in the present age, but also in the one to come.'*
> Ephesians 1:20–21 NIV

The question needs to be asked:

Over which powers did Christ establish his authority? Did he disarm the demonic powers, or was it the structural powers that he defeated?

The answer is both!

He disarmed the devil (Hebrews 2:14) and his devilish powers, that Paul calls *'the spiritual forces of evil in the heavenly realms.'* (Ephesians 6:12 NIV).

He also disarmed the rebellion of the earthly powers, *'the rulers, the authorities, the powers of this dark world'* (Ephesians 6:12 NIV) They too are subject to his authority and his lordship.

> *'Then Jesus came to them and said, "All authority in heaven and on earth has been given to me"'* Matthew 28:18 NIV

That authority is creation-wide, it is both temporal and eternal, it is both spiritual and natural, it is over the 'all things' of creation and the 'all things' of redemption. That means that not only do the demonic powers have to yield to Christ's authority, but the structural powers also have to yield to his lordship. And we invested with the authority of the Risen Lord and empowered to press the claims of that Lordship, are called to enter the city, the realm of the powers.

Chapter 19

The City Revisited

What we have covered briefly so far is an essential foundation to enable Christians to live freely, victoriously and creatively in the structures of a secular society and within the influence of the antagonistic powers that are there. But we are called, not merely to survive successfully in this milieu, we are called to do something about the powers themselves so that through us the manifold wisdom of God may be made known to them. (Ephesians 3:10) To do so, we need to revisit the city in the light of what we have learned. Note the following very important points.

1. The structural entity, the corporate spirit that we call the 'city' or the 'power', is fallen but not demonic. Because of its fallenness it is both dominating and potentially idolatrous, but it is still the object of redemption. Therefore, we are not to reject or fear it, or withdraw from it. We are to care for and rebuild it, and recover it to acknowledge the Lordship of Jesus Christ and to serve him.

2. Regardless of the fallenness and dominance of structural powers Christians can live within their environment, and serve their legitimate goals without submitting to their claims to exercise ultimate authority. The greatest earthly power, the modern state, is never more than a penultimate authority; the ultimate authority is always Jesus Christ. When we are under his ultimate authority we have an inner freedom from all other

idolatrous claims. That inner freedom, which is our right as believers is real, it is guaranteed by Jesus Christ and we are meant to experience it. When we do, it will affect our inner attitudes and our outward actions, whether we are the CEO of the corporation or the lowliest employee, the senior pastor of the church or the humblest member.

3. The character of the power is in its beginnings relatively plastic, that is it is formed and shaped either deliberately or unconsciously by its founders. As it progresses it gathers a life and character of its own, becomes more resistant to change, and exercises its own shaping influence on those within its realm. Nevertheless it always retains a certain malleability, that is to say its character can be modified or changed by strong leaders, by influential participants, or by momentous or decisive events. This means that in an organisation such as a church, for example, we can either deliberately seek to create the character we want, or we can just let it happen like careless parents who allow their children to grow up anyhow and be shaped by whatever influences come their way. We do not admire or approve of parents like that.

4. We have seen that behind the structural powers of the world system there is a demonic overlay, called the 'rulers of this age.' (1 Corinthians 2:6, 8; Ephesians 6:12) These demonic powers reinforce the rebellion of the structural powers and seek to set them in concrete so that they will refuse to change in the direction of righteousness. More than policy change is needed, what is required is character change, and that is a moral/spiritual issue.

5. As Christians we therefore face action in relation to the powers on two fronts:

(a) Casting down demonic strongholds over the powers so as to unlock them and open them up to the possibility of change. This is the realm of spiritual warfare and deliverance. It is one thing to cast demons out of people, it is another, and even more important thing to cast demons out of structures. It may involve public exorcism.

    This level of action comes first. Jesus always put first

things first. He said, first tie up the strong man and then you can rob his house. (Mark 3:27) If we do not deal effectively in prayer with this level of opposition our change efforts will undoubtedly end in frustration or worse.

(b) Addressing the structural powers and calling them back to acknowledge the One they belong to, Jesus Christ the Lord, and to fulfil their rightful destiny which is to be ministers of God for good (Romans 13:4) and part of the economy of creation that will ultimately be summed up under the headship of Christ. (Ephesians 1:10) This is the realm of influence and redemptive organisational change and it is every bit as important as spiritual warfare. The two must go hand in hand for if we do not become actively involved in working for change in the structures, all our spiritual warfare will be unproductive or even counterproductive, as Jesus warned in Matthew 12:43–45. What is usually overlooked in this passage is that Jesus applied the analogy of the re-demonised individual to describe the state of an entire society.

Changing the structural powers in the direction of righteousness is rebuilding the ruined city:

> *They will rebuild the ancient ruins,*
> *and restore the places long devastated;*
> *they will renew the ruined cities*
> *that have been devastated for generations.*
> *Aliens will shepherd your flocks;*
> *foreigners will work your fields and vineyards.*
> *And you will be called the priests of the Lord,*
> *You will be named ministers of our God.*
>
> Isaiah 61:4–6 NIV

Organisational Change Agent – Nehemiah

A detailed biblical blueprint for organisational change can be found in the book of Nehemiah. It has particular relevance to our present subject because while the book of Ezra deals with the rebuilding of the temple, Nehemiah deals with the rebuilding of the city. In Nehemiah's day the temple had been rebuilt for 70 years but the city was still in ruins. God's order, it seems, is first the temple, then the city. In the last 30 years or so we have seen in the charismatic renewal a substantial rebuilding of the temple, that is, the church. But society is in ruins. That is where the focus of God's attention lies today.

Here then is a summary of Nehemiah's method, it has widespread application to the 'cities' in which we live and work today.

1. Care for the city.

'When I heard these words I sat down and wept and mourned for days' (Nehemiah 1:4 Amplified) John Greenleaf says that the problem with our society today is that nobody loves the institutions. He is right and this I fear, is particularly true of us Christians. We fear and dislike the structural powers, we are both overawed and repelled by them, we submit to them and sometimes realise that we are being seduced by them and bought by them. We rail against their evil, criticise and condemn their failings, but we do not care for them, and care is nothing less than love in action. If we are ever going to change our organisation we need to feel towards it, the way the Jew felt towards Jerusalem –

> *If I forget you, O Jerusalem,*
> *may my right hand forget its skill.*
> *May my tongue cling to the roof of my mouth,*
> *if I do not remember you,*
> *if I do not consider Jerusalem*
> *my highest joy.*   Psalm 137:5–6 NIV

2. Pray for the city.

'For some days I mourned and fasted and prayed before the God of heaven…' (Nehemiah 1:4–11 NIV) Nehemiah's prayer, which ought to be read and pondered by every leader, includes two valuable insights for organisational change agents.

(a) He identified himself with the sin of the city. *'I confess the sins we Israelites, including myself and my father's house have committed against you.'* (Nehemiah 1:6 NIV) In dealing with the powers we are involved with corporate structures and with corporate evil and because we are part of those structures we share an inescapable corporate responsibility for what is wrong and what has gone wrong.

(b) He was willing to become part of the answer to his own prayer. (Nehemiah 1:11) Genuine intercession very often leads to intervention, but genuine intercession always requires the willingness to be the one who intervenes.

3. Plan for the city.

A period of about four months elapsed between the events of chapter 1 and those of chapter 2 of Nehemiah. What was going on in that period comes out in the course of Nehemiah's interview with the king and queen. What he asked for then, was not the result of instant inspiration but the fruit of weeks of prayer and careful deliberation. What he came up with was not a detailed set of plans, it was something more important:

(a) He got the big vision.

What 50,000 Jews under Zerubbabel had failed in 70 years to accomplish, Nehemiah decided to tackle. When he thought about Jerusalem he decided, 'I will rebuild it'. With the big vision came the bold request, nothing less than asking for the governorship of Judea to enable him to do the job. (Nehemiah 2:7–8). To succeed, movements must always go for radical rather than cosmetic change.

(b) The long term goal.

The king asked Nehemiah how long he would be away and when he would return and Nehemiah 'set a time.' (Nehemiah 2:6) If you compare chapter 2:1 and chapter 13:6 you will find that the time was 12 years.

Institutional change takes time and the more radical the reordering is, the slower is the process. Therefore, to succeed, we have to be committed for the long haul.

4. Live in the city.

A culture, whether that of a society or that of an organisation, can generally be changed only from the inside. With a true instinct for what was involved, Nehemiah came and lived in the city (Nehemiah 2:11) Even if you are an external change agent, in a consultancy role for example, you have to get 'in', you have to get inside the organisation before you can effectively change it in a way that does not damage its spirit. The requirements for getting in will include amongst other things a respectful, non judgmental and humble willingness to learn the ways of the city and share in its life.

5. Research the city and know its real problems.

By the time Nehemiah had been in Jerusalem for less than a week he already knew the city and its problems better than any of the people who had lived there for years. (Nehemiah 2:11)

(a) He saw the whole picture and the total extent of the problem with the objectivity and fresh eyes of a newcomer.

(b) He examined it personally and at first hand so he could make his own mind up about it without the excuses and rationalisations of the inhabitants.

(c) He saw the problems from a particular perspective, that is, from the perspective of someone who believed they could be solved and intended to do something about it.

6. Start a movement.

There is ample evidence to show that social transformation, whether it is in a culture or in the life of an organisation is usually accomplished by a 'movement' which has the specific aim of bringing about the changes that are considered neces-sary. Furthermore it has been established that the most power-ful movements are always those that are;

(a) Conceptually radical, and

(b) Based on a religious type commitment.

A movement does not require a majority in favour of it before it can be launched. It is the type of social change that can be initiated by a dedicated minority but once a movement has achieved a life of its own it can be stopped only by complete and crushing force. What we find Nehemiah doing is initiating just such a movement. Here is his strategy, which can be applied to small and large scale organisations alike:

(a) Find the influencers. (ch 2:16) Nehemiah got hold of the small number of key people in the city whose views counted, the opinion leaders, the trend setters, those whom other people followed.

(b) Get them to face the problem. (ch 2:17) Nehemiah spelled it out for them the way he saw it, *'Jerusalem lies in ruins'* it is a wasteland, a reproach, a disgrace. But he made it clear that it was his problem as much as theirs. He did not say, 'You see the trouble you are in,' he said 'You see the trouble we are in'. This identification of the change agent with the problem is very important.

(c) Give them a vision; *'Come let us rebuild the walls of Jerusalem and we will no longer be in disgrace.'* Nehemiah emphasised the possibilities; the job, he said, can be done, it is within our capacity to accomplish it. But note that Nehemiah was not just talking vision. He was a born leader, and he knew the territory in which leaders work – he had already made some of the crucial decisions that would pull the vision from the future into the present. (see Nehemiah 2:7)

> *'I also told them about the gracious hand of my God upon me and what the king had said to me.'* Nehemiah 2:18 NIV

(d) Get them to buy into the vision for themselves. *'Then they replied "Let us start rebuilding"'* (ch 2:18) This is the critical point in any movement for change. It has to be owned by those who will run with it, it is no longer the leaders' vision, it is the vision of the movement. The leader or the initiator of the vision has ultimately to let it go as his or her personal preserve so that it becomes the property of the movement. If the leader insists on holding on to a proprietory claim to the movement because he or she brought it to birth, it will be crippled from the start. Fewer will join it, fewer still will sacrifice for it and stick with it in hard times, and fewer still will be faithful to it if the founder leaves, dies, or loses interest.

7. Foster the growth of the movement for change.
Participation in a movement generally has characteristics that the leader needs to identify or initiate and then to foster.

(a) Personal commitment by a core of individuals who believe they can change their immediate surroundings or environment.

(b) Recruitment of friends or colleagues to join in small scale efforts, or what I call, 'winnable opportunities.' The most successful movements usually develop a track record of small but observable successes in changing things until gradually they accumulate growing support. The rebuilding in Nehemiah 3 has all the characteristics of a spontaneous, small scale, localised movement for change that gradually gained momentum as more people joined in with something that was actually achieving results.

(c) Development of flexible, cell-like, non bureaucratic structures that can be created, adapted, altered and dissolved as required. What seems, in Nehemiah 3, like a loose jumble of ad hoc groupings with little consistent structure about them, was just that. But it got the job done.

(d) Expectation of and willingness to face opposition from the establishment. When a movement is under way, the interesting thing is that opposition and attack from the establishment only strengthens its resolve. (Nehemiah 2:20, 4:1ff)

(e) The willingness to go for radical or fundamental rather than peripheral change, and the ability to discern the difference. Nehemiah faced not only the threat of violent opposition but also the more subtle distraction of the offer of negotiations with his opponents. (Nehemiah 6:1–9)

8. Reiterate, reinforce and restate the goals as required along the way.

Even when change is actually under way the work of the leaders is not finished.

(a) The vision has to be repeated, and the aims and ideals have to be articulated and expressed in ways that are appropriate to each stage of the movement's development or history.

(b) People have to be continuously encouraged, motivated, corrected and sometimes disciplined (Nehemiah 4:14, 5:1–13).

(c) Difficulties have to be faced, problems solved and the movement represented to the outside world. (Nehemiah 4:16–20)

9. Finally along with and even after the rebuilding there is the on-going process of re-educating and re-ordering the inner life of the city.

The first six chapters of Nehemiah deal with the rebuilding of the walls of Jerusalem, the next six chapters deal with the even more difficult task of reforming its character. The last chapter is a timely warning that the task is never complete in this age and backsliding into the old ways is an ever present danger.

Chapter 20

When Leaders Fail

The possession of leadership gifts and capabilities no more guarantees that a leader will never fail than the possession of managerial abilities automatically protects from the chance of business collapse or sporting abilities mean that you will never be beaten. Therefore from time to time leaders fail, and sometimes fail badly. The percentage who do so is probably no higher than in any other activity but such failures tend to attract more attention because a leader's role is a highly visible one and a leader's downfall generally affects the lives and interests of numbers of people.

The critical issue however is not the condemnation but the recovery and restoration of leaders who fail, a work that the church has generally done very badly. It has been accused, not without some justification, of being an army that shoots its wounded. Restoration of fallen leaders is however of prime importance, not only because it is the compassionate or redemptive thing to do, but because failure can be a crucial stage on the pathway to a leader's real usefulness. This I know at first hand. Failure is the drastic surgery God sometimes has to use to cut the stubborn nerve of self sufficiency in a leader's life. When that happens we may, in a sense, go limping ever after but the truth is that we have at long last begung to change from being Jacob, the supplanter, dependant on guile and astute gamesmanship, to Israel, a prince with God.

How Leaders Fail

Let it be clear that what we are addressing here is not the ordinary occasions where leaders make mistakes or errors of judgment. No leaders are exempt from these. What we are dealing with are those situations where actions or omissions on the part of leaders have resulted in serious or irretrievable failure or breakdown. The circumstances in which these catastrophes happen will vary widely. They can all be generally classified under the following headings:

Failures where no moral blame or censure is involved

1. Cases where persons who are not leaders have been placed in leadership roles and have therefore found the requirements of the position more than they can handle.

2. Cases where the persons have leadership capabilities but the demands of the particular appointment have been beyond their ability or knowledge or experience. In other words the leaders are just out of their depth.

3. Cases where the leaders have made very serious errors of judgment or repeated mistakes so that the people have lost all confidence in their ability to lead.

Failure where moral blame or censure is involved

4. Cases where leaders have treated people unjustly or unfairly or have been guilty of serious breaches of confidence so that people have lost confidence in their integrity.

5. Cases where leaders in a team have fallen out with one another and instead of settling their differences they have allowed their disputes to weaken or divide the people in the church or organisation.

6. Cases where leaders have failed morally in their private or personal lives.

The Restoration of Leaders who have Failed

It will be clear from even a cursory examination of the headings above that quite different issues are involved in each type of failure and therefore the remedial work that has to be undertaken will also differ. The best way of dealing with this is to discuss each class briefly.

1. Non-leaders trying to lead.

The problem here is simply job mismatch. Research has clearly established that a person's strengths and motivations are innate, that is, they are placed there by God from birth and cannot basically be altered in nature although they can be developed or frustrated. In other words all of us are made to be good at some things but not good at everything. If we are in a position that requires strengths or motivations different from those we possess, we will always feel under pressure, will never produce more than mediocre results and will always be liable to fail. That is sadly true of many gifted people in organisations who are snared by the stereotype that the only ladder to climb is the ladder of leadership. People without the capacities for leadership find their motivation drained by the task and at the same time their real strengths and giftings that lie elsewhere become frustrated. The task of restoration for people wounded by the experience of failure will involve attending to the following areas.

(a) Helping the persons concerned to realise the reasons for what has happened so that they can be released from the sense of failure and guilt. They have been struggling to fulfil a role that they were never meant to tackle.

It is very likely that their self confidence and sense of self worth will also have taken a beating and they need to be reassured of these by people who genuinely accept and respect them and care for their welfare.

(b) Obtaining an accurate description of the person's strengths and motivations. This is best undertaken professionally with a process such as S.I.M.A., the System for Identifying Motivated Abilities developed by Arther Millar. This unique system which is conceptually compatible with the biblical view of man is now validated by over 35,000 case studies and has been of inestimable value in

214

identifying problems caused by job mismatch and in giving advice on career choice and career redirection.

(c) Having found the shape of the person's strengths and motivations, helping them to get launched in an area of service or ministry that fits these strengths and will bring them both joy and fulfilment.

2. and 3. Leaders who make serious errors of judgement.

These cases are similar except that No. 2 is more excusable because an inexperienced leader has been given too much responsibility too soon or has been faced with decisions and problems that he or she does not yet have enough training or skill or experience to deal with. In both cases however, wisdom and compassion are needed so that potentially useful leadership careers are not shipwrecked. The situations require:

(a) A careful analysis of the reasons underlying the failures and a clear understanding and acceptance by the leaders concerned as to how they have gone wrong. This requires both honesty and humility on the part of those who have made the mistakes.

(b) A strategy to deal with both the immediate and the longer term consequences as far as the organisation or group is concerned so that effects of the failure can be corrected and the position retrieved if at all possible.

(c) Plans to remedy the inadequacies as far as the leaders are concerned. These may include:

(i) Training or mentoring by more experienced leaders.

(ii) The building of a team around an isolated leader so that the task can be coped with.

(iii) Leaders who are out of their depth moving back to a level of responsibility more in keeping with their ability and experience so that they can regain confidence and credibility.

(d) Providing ongoing pastoral care of leaders so that they have access to other leaders with whom they can freely discuss difficulties, challenges and achievements. This ensures that problems are faced before they become major headaches.

Pastoral care should also extend to assist in rebuilding other areas of leaders' lives that have suffered because of the stress of failure, for example marriage and family relationships.

(e) The sharing of all these plans and courses of action with the people so that they can express their love for and affirmation of the leader as a person and feel that they have a part in the restoration. There should also be the opportunity for wrong feelings and critical attitudes to be put right on both sides.

4, 5 and 6. Where moral failure is evident.

These three cases involve different dynamics because areas of moral wrongdoing have occurred. Other factors such as those in cases 1 to 3 may also be there in which cases the steps outlined above will also apply. We will deal specifically here with the moral issues that have to be handled, they are:

1. Repentance.
2. Restitution.
3. Reordering.

Repentance.

Gipsy Smith the famous English evangelist of some generations ago used to declare that all the problems of the Christian life are due to inadequate repentance. Whether his assessment is accurate or not, we need to underscore the fact that repentance is more than an apology or an expression of regret for what has happened. It requires a certain clear understanding by the offending parties of what has actually occurred and what is to be done about it. These matters are not to be fudged or hurried over on the assumption that Christians and particularly Christian leaders understand all there is about repentance. Experience, including experience with our own hearts will soon convince us that this is far from the case.

For true repentance there has to be:

(a) A sincere acknowledgment that the law of God that has been broken is a righteous law and that it was wrong to break it.

(b) A sincere acknowledgment of personal guilt in breaking the law, without excuse or rationalisation.

(c) A sincere intention to amend, and to be odedient in the future to the law that has been broken.

The other, equally important aspect is that there is faith that the offended party is willing to forgive and that they forgive, not only as ones who have suffered personal injury but also as ones who righteously resent the offence committed against the law of God in their person.

The question of forgiveness is often as little understood as the question of repentance and this will usually have to be taught also. For the wrongdoing to be adequately dealt with the offender not only has to offer sincere repentance but must be able to believe that the one who forgives, in doing so still preserves a true regard for the law of God that has been violated. This means that the offer of repentance must never be allowed to be dismissed with, 'Never mind, it doesn't really matter'.

Restitution.

This may seem a difficult and even outmoded concept to raise but it is of vital importance, not to the question of forgiveness so much as to the matter of restoration. The key passage is Leviticus 6:2–6 which provides that, if a person sins and acts unfaithfully against the Lord by deceiving his neighbour about something entrusted to him or left in his care, or if he cheats him, or if he swears falsely,

217

(a) He must return what was entrusted to him, or whatever it was he swore falsely about

(b) He must make restitution in full, add a fifth in value to it, and give it all to the owner on the day he presents his guilt offering

(c) He must bring to the priest, that is to the Lord, his guilt offering and the priest will make atonement for him and he will be forgiven.

Restitution is not earning forgiveness but it is making amends for the wrong done. It may involve a public apology to a person who has been unjustly treated, or it may involve voluntarily undertaking a servant role towards people who have been treated arrogantly or have been dominated. Its purpose is, as far as it is possible to undo the wrong that has been done, so that the law of God is upheld and shalom is restored.

The purpose is therefore neither punishment on the one hand or earning forgiveness on the other, it is the restoration of relationships. Ideally the action that is taken should arise out of a mutual agreement between the parties as to what is appropriate under the circumstances. It may be that nothing more than repentance and forgiveness is needed to restore shalom, it may be that some form of recompense or restitution is valid and necessary for the sake of both parties.

Reordering.

Another vital aspect of restoration, that is too often neglected entirely or drastically skimped, is the willingness on the part of leaders who have failed to spend time rebuilding the areas of their lives that have proven to be flawed. Time alone will not do it, a more deliberate discipline is almost always necessary even though it is a painful process to go through.

> 'No discipline seems pleasant at the time, but painful. Later on, however, it produces a harvest of righteousness and peace for those who have been trained by it.'   Hebrews 12:11 NIV

The work of aiding in the restoration of a leader requires qualities of wisdom, compassion and patience and above all the heart of a father, who is willing to minister discipline firmly but fairly and lovingly and who rejoices when it is all over. In dealing with a leader in this situation the specific areas of failure have to be addressed to discover:

1. What is the nature of the failure? What happened?

There may be one major and obvious error that has brought disaster or it may be a tangled skein of inadequacies or misjudgments in a number of areas that need to be patiently unravelled to establish the facts. This probing and analysis must not be hurried and must be worked through as objectively and dispassionately as possible. You will ordinarily find that you are up against a great amount of confusion in the mind of the leader, as well as unconscious defence mechanisms that can make it impossible for him to see the issues with any degree of clarity.

2. What is the cause of the failure? Why did it happen?

This area requires even greater care and insight because now you are probing for causation. Why did the leader make such serious errors of judgment? Is she prone to jump to conclusions without sufficient consideration? Does he make snap judgments to impress others with his decisiveness? Does he panic under pressure or get flustered when there are too many options to choose from?

Why did the leader act so unfairly towards certain people? Does he have long standing prejudices against certain personalities or certain types? Does she react to criticism by personal attack? If so why? Does he carry grudges or find it hard to put up with people who are slow to learn new things?

Does the failure show up serious character flaws that need to be addressed? Are there problems with lust, or anger, or untruthfulness? Are there marriage problems that are not being dealt with? Does the leader have an inordinate desire to be accepted, or loved, or admired?

The aim in all of this is to enable the leader not only to understand for himself what the problems are that have to be faced, but also to have the courage to address the problems and the confidence that they can be overcome.

3. How can the cause or causes of failure be corrected?

This may mean going beyond understanding the causes to developing specific strategies to enable dangerous or unhelpful patterns of behaviour to be discarded and new and more helpful or consistent patterns learned. Or it may be that extensive ministry is needed for emotional or inner healing or to break bondages or ties whose existence has been disclosed. The essential thing is that it must go beyond the level of understanding to the level of remedial action.

The course of action should be fully discussed and mutually agreed upon. Willing participation in it is essential for success.

4. How can we know that the weakness or failure has been corrected and that the leader can begin to function with some confidence in those areas again?

There is no ready rule of thumb answer to this question. Time must be allowed, not only for the leader's commitment to the prescribed courses of action to take effect, but also for the governmental dealings of God in his or her life.

Encouragement will be needed and the recognition of progress being made. What the leader needs is the presence of an affirming friend who is still objective enough to resist impatience and insist on the job being done properly. It is indeed a mark of a genuine work of God in a person's life when they are willing to wait patiently for the release to be given rather than to strive for it. No one who cares enough for the leader to walk through these valleys with him will want to endanger the result by too early exposure to a public role again. Nor however will they want release to be delayed unduly because the mentoring role is an extremely demanding one.

Objectives
of the
Kapiti Christian Centre

The following goals and objectives have been
accepted for the life of our Christian community.

All the activities in which we engage
should relate in some way to these goals.

Objectives for our Corporate Life

1. The fostering of real fellowship and relatedness amongst all members.
2. The expression of true Body life and ministry in meetings.
3. Development and growth in the expression of corporate worship.

Objectives for Individual Life

4. The encouragement of personal spiritual growth and maturity in members.
5. Assistance in the discovery and exercise of individual gifts and ministries.
6. The enlargement of opportunities for influence and participation in the life of the church community.

Objectives for Outreach

7. Evangelism – reaching and winning others to Christ.
8. Leading Christians into the experience of the baptism in the Holy Spirit and the walk in the Spirit.
9. Ministering to human needs at every level.
10. Seeking to fellowship with all the Body of Christ.
11. Supporting missionary endeavour and inculcating a missionary vision.

The Elders, Kapiti Christian Centre